John Stevens

# Business Grammar

## no problem

### Eine Englischgrammatik mit Übungen und Tests

**Cornelsen**

**Business Grammar – no problem**
*Eine Englischgrammatik mit Übungen und Tests*

**Verfasser**
*John Stevens*

**Berater**
*John Eastwood, Christine House*

**Redaktion**
*Sigrid Janssen*

**Projektleitung**
*Murdo MacPhail*

**Umschlaggestaltung**
*werkstatt für gebrauchsgrafik, Berlin*

**Layout & Technische Umsetzung**
*Stephan Hilleckenbach, Berlin*

**www.cornelsen.de**

1. Auflage, 4. Druck 2017

© 2010 Cornelsen Verlag, Berlin
© 2017 Cornelsen Verlag GmbH, Berlin

Druck und Bindung: Livonia Print, Riga

ISBN 978-3-06-520623-5

**PEFC zertifiziert**
Dieses Produkt stammt aus nachhaltig
bewirtschafteten Wäldern und kontrollierten
Quellen.

www.pefc.de

PEFC/12-31-006

## Grammatik flexibel lernen, üben, wiederholen

**Business Grammar – no problem** ist eine Übungsgrammatik, mit der die wichtigsten Strukturen der englischen Grundgrammatik gelernt, geübt und gefestigt werden können. Das Buch ist speziell auf die Bedürfnisse von Lernenden ausgerichtet, die Englisch im Beruf benötigen, und geht auf typische Fehler ein, die immer wieder bei deutschen Muttersprachlern vorkommen.

### Inhalt und Aufbau

**Business Grammar – no problem** enthält 48 Lektionen, die alle wichtigen Grammatikthemen abdecken. Jede Lektion ist als übersichtliche Doppelseite angelegt – auf der linken Seite finden Sie Erklärungen mit Beispielsätzen und auf der rechten Seite Übungen.

Jede linke Seite wird mit einem kurzen Ausschnitt aus einem beruflichen Dialog oder Text eröffnet, der typische Fehler bewusst macht und korrigiert. Danach folgen Beispiele und Erläuterungen auf Deutsch zum Gebrauch der Struktur. Das Symbol ❗ weist dabei auf besondere Fehlerquellen hin. Am Fuß der Seite wird unter **Das Wichtigste in Kürze** noch einmal alles zusammengefasst.

Auf der rechten Seite finden Sie abwechslungsreiche Übungen mit ansteigendem Schwierigkeitsgrad: Fehleranalyse, praktische Anwendung, Übersetzung. Der beigelegte Lösungsschlüssel hilft Ihnen, Ihre Eingaben zu kontrollieren.

Ab Seite 102 finden Sie zwölf Tests, mit denen Sie Ihren Lernerfolg kontrollieren können. Der Anhang ab Seite 120 bietet nützliche Hinweise und weitere Hilfen (Näheres im Inhaltsverzeichnis auf den Seiten 4 und 5). Auf der Umschlagklappe hinten finden Sie eine Übersicht der wichtigsten unregelmäßigen Verben, die Sie heraustrennen und als Lesezeichen benutzen können.

### Die Arbeit mit dem Buch

**Business Grammar – no problem** ist flexibel einsetzbar und dient der Einführung und Einübung neuer Grammatikstrukturen und/oder der Wiederholung und Vertiefung. Das Buch kann im Unterricht und/oder für das Selbststudium eingesetzt werden.
Die Lektionen müssen nicht der Reihe nach durchgearbeitet werden, sondern Sie können Schwerpunkte setzen. In den einzelnen Lektionen finden Sie Hinweise auf andere Kapitel, in denen ähnliche oder weiterführende Themen behandelt werden.

- Im Inhaltsverzeichnis können Sie sich orientieren und das Thema bestimmen, das Sie bearbeiten wollen.
- Lesen Sie die kurze Einleitung in den Units und denken Sie über die dort aufgezeigten typischen Fehler nach.
- Arbeiten Sie die Beispielsätze und deutschen Erklärungen durch. Machen Sie anschließend die Übungen.
- Kontrollieren Sie Ihre Lösungen mit Hilfe des Lösungsschlüssels.
- Wenn Sie Fehler gemacht haben, lesen Sie die Erklärungen noch einmal durch.
- Und wenn Sie das Gefühl haben, dass alles „sitzt", kontrollieren Sie Ihren Lernerfolg mit dem entsprechenden Test.

# 1 Simple present
## Einfache Gegenwart

**works** **doesn't work**
Ed ~~work~~ in logistics. He ~~doesn't works~~ in sales.

**What does logistics mean?**
~~What means logistics?~~

## Form

- **he/she/it mit -s** — Ann travels a lot. She enjoys it. *Ann reist viel. Sie genießt es.*

- **Verneinung mit don't und doesn't** — I don't work on Mondays. *Montags arbeite ich nicht.*
The company doesn't pay well. *Das Unternehmen zahlt nicht gut.*

- **Fragen mit do und does** — Do managers eat in the canteen? *Essen Manager in der Kantine?*
When does the canteen open? *Wann macht die Kantine auf?*

- **Kurzantworten mit do und does (+ not)** — Do they know? – Yes, they do. / No, they don't. *Wissen sie es? – Ja./Nein.*
Does it cost a lot? – Yes, it does. / No, it doesn't. *Kostet es viel? – Ja./Nein.*

## Gebrauch

- **Feststehende Tatsachen** — Factories need energy. *Fabriken brauchen Energie.*

- **Gewohnheiten** — I usually leave the house at 7 o'clock. *Ich verlasse das Haus meist um 7 Uhr.*

- **Regelmäßige Vorgänge** — The boss gets a daily report. *Der Chef bekommt einen täglichen Bericht.*

- **Berufsangaben** — My partner works for Microsoft. *Mein Partner arbeitet bei Microsoft.*

- **Hobbys und Freizeit** — Jacqui plays tennis. *Jacqui spielt Tennis.*

- **Gefühle und Meinungen** — I like the idea. What do you think? *Ich mag die Idee. Was meinen Sie?*

## Signalwörter

- **Ausdrücke der Häufigkeit** — always, usually, normally, mostly, often, sometimes, rarely, never, hardly ever, every morning/day/week/month/time/...

- **Uhr- und Tageszeiten** — at six o'clock, in the morning, at breakfast time, before/after work

- **Wochentage, Monate,** — on Monday(s), on weekdays, at the weekend, in June

- **Jahreszeiten, Feste** — in the summer, at Easter, before Christmas

## Stellung der Signalwörter

Ausdrücke der Häufigkeit (außer solchen mit every) stehen meist vor dem letzten Verbteil.
Alle anderen (einschl. Ausdrücke mit every) stehen meist am Satzende.

I don't often see Alan at work.    I see Ann every day / at lunch / on Mondays.

**!** Ein Signalwort kann **nicht** zwischen Verb und Objekt stehen!
~~I take always the 7.50 train.~~    I always take the 7.50 train.
~~I do every morning the same.~~    I do the same every morning.

**!** Ein Signalwort kann auch **nicht** zwischen Verb und adverbialer Bestimmung stehen.
~~I sleep always on the train.~~    I always sleep on the train.

## > Das Wichtigste in Kürze

- he/she/it mit -s; Frage und Verneinung mit einer Form von do
- Häufigkeitsausdrücke (außer every ...) vor dem Verb – **Kein** Signalwort zwischen Verb und Objekt!

Weitere Informationen ⟶ Units 3, 4, 14

**A** Underline the correct form.

1 What  does this word mean / means this word?
2 She  usually starts / starts usually  work at 8.
3 We  don't need often / don't often need  help.
4 Do you  always park here / park always here?
5 Where  do you live / live you?
6 I  doesn't like / don't like  my new office.
7 Mark  work / works  for a French company.
8 We  don't have / have not  a canteen.

**B** Make negative sentences.

I work from home.
**I don't work from home.**

1 I get home before 8 o'clock most days.
2 This company produces sportswear.
3 I go to work by train.
4 We usually take visitors to the canteen.
5 My colleagues travel a lot.

Now ask questions.

You / work / from home?
**Do you work from home?**

6 What time / you / get home?
7 What / your company / produce?
8 How / you / go to work?
9 Where / you / usually take visitors?
10 you and your colleagues / travel a lot?

**C** Complete these dialogues with the verbs in the correct form.

1 A: When ................................... (the meeting / start)?

B: Sorry, I ................................... (not know).

2 A: ................................... (Emma/speak) Chinese?

B: No. She ................................... (not need) it in her job.

3 A: ................................... (you/work) at the weekend?

B: I ................................... (sometimes work) on Sunday.

4 A: When ................................... (Sam/need) the data?

B: He ................................... (not need) it today.

5 A: What ................................... (the tickets / cost)?

B: $3.95. ................................... (we/have) the right coins?

**D** Give short answers.

1 Does Ann still work here? – No, ...............

2 Do you sell to China? – Yes, we ...............

3 Do Ed and Pete know? – No, ...............

4 Does Mike travel a lot? – Yes, ...............

5 Do you enjoy your work? – Yes, ...............

6 Does the service cost much? – No, ...............

**E** Make sentences with these items. There is always one part that you don't need.

1 I / late / often / on a Thursday. / work / works ...................................................................

2 at the weekend. / doesn't / not / Tony / usually / work ...................................................................

3 cost / costs / doesn't / The taxi / so much. / usually ...................................................................

4 a meeting / don't / every Monday morning. / have / not / We ...................................................................

5 always / don't / doesn't / They / give / us / all the information. ...................................................................

**F** Translate the following sentences.

1 Was bedeutet dieses Symbol?
2 Wo treffen Sie sich normalerweise?
3 Welches Design-Studio nutzen Sie?
4 Was arbeiten Sie? (= Was machen Sie beruflich?)
5 Meine Chefin mag die Idee nicht.

7

| | |
|---|---|
| *isn't coming* <br> *at home this week* <br> Mike ~~is coming not~~ today. He's working ~~this week at home~~. | *are we discussing* <br> What ~~we are discussing~~ today? |

### Form

| | |
|---|---|
| ■ Form von **be** mit Endung **-ing**\* | Leave me alone. I**'m working**. *Lass mich in Ruhe. Ich arbeite (gerade).* <br> Listen. They**'re arguing**. *Horch. Sie streiten sich.* |
| ■ Verneinung mit **be + not** | You **aren't (= are not) listening**. *Du hörst nicht zu.* <br> Oh no! The printer **isn't working**. *O je! Der Drucker funktioniert (gerade) nicht.* |
| ■ Fragebildung durch Umstellung | The boss **is speaking** to the staff. *Die Chefin spricht zum Personal.* <br> **Is** the boss **speaking** now? *Spricht jetzt die Chefin?* |
| ■ Kurzantworten mit einer Form von **be** | **Are** you coming? – Yes, I **am**. / No, I**'m not**. *Kommen Sie? – Ja./Nein.* <br> **Is** Max leaving? – Yes, he **is**. / No, he **isn't**. *Geht Max weg? – Ja./Nein.* |

\*Schreibbesonderheiten: Siehe Seite 126.

### Gebrauch

| | |
|---|---|
| ■ Ein gerade ablaufendes Geschehen | Where are you? We**'re waiting** for you. *Wo sind Sie? Wir warten auf Sie.* <br> I**'m calling** from the airport. *Ich rufe gerade vom Flughafen aus an.* <br> Tony **is** just **parking** the car. *Tony stellt gerade das Auto ab.* |
| ■ Ein unterbrochenes Geschehen | It looks as though somebody **is using** this room today. *Es sieht aus, als ob jemand den Raum heute benutzt.* <br> How **is** your meeting **going**? *Wie läuft deine Sitzung?* |
| ■ Eine vorübergehende Situation | Ann**'s working** in Berlin this week. *Ann arbeitet diese Woche in Berlin.* <br> I**'m doing** overtime this month. *Ich mache diesen Monat Überstunden.* |
| ■ Eine längerfristige Entwicklung, die noch im Gange ist | Sales in Asia **are increasing**. *Die Verkäufe in Asien nehmen zu.* <br> I**'m learning** Chinese. *Ich lerne Chinesisch.* <br> The market **is changing**. *Der Markt verändert sich.* |
| ■ Ein für die Zukunft geplantes Vorhaben | The negotiators **are meeting** again in Paris on 10th June. *Die Verhandlungsführer treffen sich wieder am 10. Juni in Paris.* |

### Signalwörter

| | |
|---|---|
| ■ Ausdrücke für „jetzt" und für nicht abgeschlossene Zeiträume | now, at the moment, just <br> today, this week, this month, this year, this summer, still |

### Stellung der Signalwörter

**just** und **still** stehen vor dem letzten Verbteil, andere Signalwörter in der Regel am Satzanfang oder -ende.

I am **just finishing** the report.      We are **still waiting** for an answer.
**At the moment** it's raining.      The oil price **is rising** again **this month**.

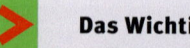

### Das Wichtigste in Kürze

- Form von **be** mit Endung **-ing**
- „Momentaufnahme" eines Ereignisses oder Vorgangs: Was geschieht gerade jetzt?

**A** **Underline the correct form.**

1 We **aren't paying** / **are paying not** much, so what can we expect?
2 I **am just downloading** / **am downloading just** the update, it's nearly finished.
3 What **you're doing** / **are you doing**?
4 They **are making today the decision** / **are making the decision today**.
5 This afternoon **are the designers giving** / **the designers are giving** their presentation.
6 I **am still trying to find** / **am trying still to find** a hotel for the conference.

**B** **Make negative sentences.**

I'm doing an online course.
**I'm not doing an online course.**

1 Maja is working in Leipzig this week.
2 We're losing customers in Europe.
3 Mr Walker is visiting Korea at the moment.
4 I'm working on Saturday this week.
5 Jason is learning Arabic.

**Now ask questions.**

What subject / you / do?
**What subject are you doing?**

6 Where / she / work?
7 Where / you / lose customers?
8 Which country / Mr Walker / visit?
9 You / work / on Sunday?
10 Which language / he / learn?

**C** **Complete these dialogues with the verbs in the correct form.**

1 A: What ................................... (you/do)?

B: I ................................... (try) to open this window.

2 A: How ................................... (we/get) into town?

B: Someone ................................... (meet) us at the airport.

3 A: They ................................... (not discuss) your paper.

B: What ................................... (they / talk about) then?

4 A: ................................... (you / wait for) Mike?

B: No, he ................................... (go) separately.

5 A: They ................................... (develop) a new model.

B: How much ................................... (they/invest)?

**D** **Make questions and give short answers.**

1 ................................... (you/enjoy) the conference? – Yes, ................., thanks. Are you?

2 ................................... (Malcolm/give) the presentation? – No, ................. . Julia is doing it.

3 ................................... (they still / fix) that software problem? – Yes, ................. .

4 ................................... (you/stay) over the weekend? – No, ................. . I have to get back.

5 ................................... (it still / rain)? – No, ................. . It's just stopped.

**E** **Translate the following sentences.**

1 Was machst du [gerade]?
2 Niemand hört mir zu!
3 Wir geben im Moment zu viel Geld aus.
4 Sam macht gerade Kopien.
5 Das Unternehmen macht immer noch keinen Gewinn.

**do you usually travel**
How ~~are you usually travelling~~ to work?

**normally walk** **am driving**
I ~~am normally walking~~. But this week I ~~drive~~.

### Einfache Gegenwart: Dauerzustand

Mit der einfachen Gegenwart beschreibt man dauerhafte Zustände, regelmäßige und sich wiederholende Vorgänge.
Es wird gesagt: Dies ist der Status quo, dies ist der Normalzustand.

- **Feststehende Tatsachen**
  I **come** from Germany. I**'m** German.

- **Gewohnheiten**
  I **don't drink** much alcohol.

- **Regelmäßige Vorgänge**
  We **meet** once a month.

- **Berufsangaben**
  Meg **teaches** English and German.

- **Hobbys und Freizeit**
  We **travel** a lot.

### Verlaufsform: Momentaner Vorgang

Mit der Verlaufsform beschreibt man einen Vorgang, der gerade im Verlauf begriffen, vorübergehend und nicht abgeschlossen ist.
Es wird gesagt: Dies passiert gerade, ist aber nur eine Momentaufnahme, nicht dauernd so.

- **Momentanes Geschehen**
  It**'s raining**.

- **Unterbrochener Vorgang**
  They**'re building** a new warehouse here, but it's Sunday today, that's why nobody **is working**.

- **Vorübergehende Situation**
  I**'m staying** at the Regent Hotel.

- **Längere, nicht abgeschlossene Entwicklung**
  Temperatures **are rising** worldwide.

### Beide Formen im Vergleich

| | |
|---|---|
| Ann **works** for an Italian company. ⋯⟩ | She **is working** on a new project now. |
| I **don't enjoy** business trips. ⋯⟩ | But I**'m enjoying** this one. |
| The conference **doesn't** normally **finish** till Friday. ⋯⟩ | But this year it**'s finishing** a day earlier. |
| Where **do** they usually **interview** people? ⋯⟩ | Why **are** they **interviewing** in a hotel this time? |
| **Does** your company **pay** for language courses? ⋯⟩ | **Is** it **paying** for this course? |

Eine feste berufliche Situation wird immer mit der einfachen Gegenwart ausgedrückt; eine vorübergehende oder nicht abgeschlossene Lern- oder Ausbildungssituation mit der Verlaufsform.

| | |
|---|---|
| Donna **works** in the automobile industry. ⋯⟩ | Her son **is studying** at a technical university. |
| She **designs** car seats. ⋯⟩ | He **is training** to be a designer. |
| She **does** interesting work. ⋯⟩ | He **is doing** a holiday job during the summer. |
| She **gets** a good salary. ⋯⟩ | He **isn't getting** much money. |

> ### Das Wichtigste in Kürze
> - Einfache Gegenwart: Etwas geschieht in bestimmten Abständen = Dauersituation/Dauerzustand
> - Verlaufsform: Etwas ist jetzt gerade im Verlauf begriffen, nicht abgeschlossen, vorübergehend

**A** **Underline the correct form.**

1 My colleague **comes** / **is coming** from the Czech Republic. She grew up in Prague.

2 We **are expanding** / **expand** into Eastern Europe. The potential market there is enormous.

3 What **are you training** / **do you train** to be? – An electrical engineer.

4 Sheila **does** / **is doing** a crash course in Portuguese before they send her to Brazil.

5 **I'm travelling** / **I travel** a lot at the moment. Too much really.

**B** **Fill in one verb in the simple present, the other in the present progressive.**

1 I usually .................... **(finish)** work at six, but this week I .................... **(work)** longer.

2 I .................... **(not come)** to the pub. I always .................... **(go)** to the sauna on Mondays.

3 Prices .................... **(rise)** fast. They usually .................... **(go up)** at this time of year.

4 Why .................... **(you/wear)** a suit today? You .................... **(not normally wear)** one.

5 I hear you .................... **(train)** to become a doctor. .................... **(doctors/earn)** much in this country?

6 The economic situation .................... **(get)** worse. But it always .................... **(get)** better after a while.

7 Who .................... **(give)** the presentation? Emma normally .................... **(do)** them.

**C** **Complete the sentences with the verbs in the correct form.**

1 Hello? Is that Marston Electronics? This is Sonja Steffen. I .................... **(call)** from Germany.

2 How often .................... **(you/check)** your emails?

3 The new model is cheaper, smaller and .................... **(use)** less electricity.

4 What's all this noise? What .................... **(you/do)**?

5 I .................... **(not work)** on Mondays, but I always have to work on Sundays.

6 Excuse me. Do you have a moment? Or .................... **(I/disturb)** you?

7 Jack's away. He .................... **(do)** a course, something that the HR department organized.

**D** **Complete these dialogues. Put the verbs in the simple present or the present progressive.**

1 A: Rachel and Martin .................... **(not speak)** to each other at the moment.

  B: I know, and the conflict .................... **(escalate)**. We can't let the situation continue.

2 A: Oh no. The restaurant .................... **(just close)**.

  B: They .................... **(not usually close)** so early.

3 A: Please be quiet. I .................... **(try)** to concentrate.

  B: I'm sorry, but I .................... **(look for)** my keys. I thought they might be here.

**E** **Translate the following sentences.**

1 [Die] Preise steigen wieder.

2 Sprichst du Spanisch? Ich lerne es gerade.

3 Die Firma baut eine neue Fabrik in Polen.

4 Ein neues Projekt fängt gerade an. Das bedeutet immer viel Arbeit.

5 Fionas Tochter spielt drei Instrumente. Sie studiert Musik.

> are thinking          depend
> We ~~think~~ about some changes. But they ~~are depending~~ on several factors.

### Verben, die normalerweise nicht in der Verlaufsform gebraucht werden

Verben, die einen Zustand (keine Tätigkeit) bezeichnen, stehen in der Regel nicht in der Verlaufsform.
Es gibt Ausnahmen, man vermeidet jedoch Fehler, wenn man diese Verben nur in der einfachen Form gebraucht.

| | |
|---|---|
| ■ Verben des Wollens, Brauchens und Mögens | Who **wants** coffee? I **need** some. I **love** coffee. |
| ■ Verben des Meinens, Wissens, Glaubens | I **think** Ed is right, but I **don't know**. I **believe** him. |
| ■ Verben, die Besitz und Wert ausdrücken | Who **owns** this? What **does** it **cost**? |
| ■ Verben des Seins, Scheinens und Bestehens | This **seems** unusual. What **does** it **consist of**? |
| ■ Verben der Sinneswahrnehmung | This **looks**, **tastes** and **smells** very strange. |
| ■ Verben des Bedeutens | What **does** this **mean**? **Does** it **matter**? |

| | | | |
|---|---|---|---|
| **be** sein | **feel** glauben; sich (an)fühlen | **matter** etwas ausmachen | **see** verstehen; sehen |
| **believe** glauben | **hate** hassen | **mean** bedeuten | **seem** erscheinen |
| **belong to** gehören | **have** haben | **need** brauchen | **smell** riechen |
| **consist of** bestehen aus | **hear** hören | **owe** schulden | **sound** sich anhören |
| **cost** kosten | **include** einschließen | **own** besitzen | **taste** schmecken |
| **depend on** abhängen von | **know** wissen; kennen | **possess** besitzen | **think** meinen |
| **doubt** bezweifeln | **like** mögen | **prefer** vorziehen | **understand** verstehen |
| **exist** existieren | **look** aussehen | **realize** erkennen | **want** wollen |
| **expect** annehmen | **love** lieben | **remember** sich erinnern | **wish** wünschen |

■ Einige dieser Verben (z. B. have, think, see, expect, be, look) haben mehr als eine Bedeutung.
In einer Bedeutung ist nur die einfache Form möglich, in einer anderen auch die Verlaufsform.

| **Zustand: keine Verlaufsform** | **Tätigkeit: Verlaufsform möglich** |
|---|---|
| I **have** no time now. *(haben)* | I **am having** a break/holiday/rest.<br>*(eine Pause/Urlaub machen / sich ausruhen)* |
| Ann **has** a lot of work just now. *(haben)* | They **are having** lunch/coffee. *(essen/trinken)* |
| Tom **has** a nice boss. *(haben)* | They **are having** a chat/talk/discussion / an argument.<br>*(sich unterhalten / diskutieren / streiten)* |
| I **have** a good feeling. *(haben)* | I'm **having** a look now. *(sich anschauen)* |
| Can I **have** a copy, please? *(haben)* | The changes **are having** an effect. *(sich auswirken)* |
| What **does** Don **think**? *(meinen)* | Quiet! He **is thinking**. *(nachdenken)* |
| We **think** the plan is good. *(meinen)* | We **are thinking** of changes. *(sich überlegen)* |
| I **see** where the mistake is. *(wahrnehmen)* | I **am seeing** Jim next Monday. *(treffen)* |
| I **see** what you're trying to say. *(verstehen)* | We're **seeing** more online sales. *(erleben)* |
| I **expect** you're tired. *(annehmen)* | I'm **expecting** a call from Tokyo. *(erwarten)* |
| Mrs Smith **is** very nice. *(sein)* | Mr Smith **is being** unhelpful. *(sein = sich verhalten)* |
| This text **looks** difficult. *(aussehen)* | What **are** you **looking** at? *(schauen)* |

>
>
> **Das Wichtigste in Kürze**
> ■ Keine Verlaufsform bei Verben, die keine Tätigkeit, sondern einen Zustand ausdrücken
> ■ Bei Verben mit mehreren Bedeutungen – Zustand: keine Verlaufsform; Tätigkeit: Verlaufsform möglich

**A** Underline the correct form.

1 Are you OK? What  **are you thinking  /  do you think**  about?
2 You  **aren't seeming  /  don't seem**  very happy. Is there a problem?
3 Maxine  **doesn't want  /  isn't wanting**  to take the job.
4 The canteen coffee  **is tasting  /  tastes**  like washing-up water!
5 **I'm seeing  /  I see**  now what the cause of the problem is.

**B** Is the form correct? If not, correct it.

1 Mr Waites **looks** stressed.
2 Why **are you having** another argument?
3 What **are you feeling** we should do next?
4 Did you read this? It **is sounding** interesting. What **are you thinking** of this?

**C** Complete the sentences with the verbs in the correct form.

1 You ............................. (have) a lovely office.

2 I ........................... (expect) you'd like a cup of coffee now.

3 Why ........................................ (you/look) there? The projector is not in that cupboard.

4 It ............................. (not matter) how much it ........................ (cost). We must have it.

5 ........................................ (you/realize) how much we have already spent on this project?

6 I ........................... (not understand) what their marketing person .................... (try) to say.

7 At first I thought she was crazy, but now I ............................. (believe) her story.

**D** Complete these dialogues. Put the verbs in the simple present or the present progressive.

1 A: Who ............................. (own) the company now?

   B: I ............................. (think) it ............................. (belong to) a Chinese consortium.

2 A: I now ........................... (realize) why they ........................... (not want) to invest

   at the moment. Somebody ........................... (take) us over.

   B: What? I ........................... (not think) that I ........................... (understand) you.

3 A: ........................... (you/take) the day off tomorrow?

   B: It ........................... (depend on) the boss, but I ............................. (doubt) it.

4 A: I'm sorry, I ........................... (feel) that I ........................... (owe) you an apology.

   B: Really? What for? I ......................... (not remember) anything.

5 A: It ........................... (seem) that they ........................... (need) you tomorrow.

   B: Why ............................. (they/have) another meeting? I can't go. You .....................

   (know) how full my schedule is. I really ............................. (have) no time at all.

**E** Translate the following sentences.

1 Wem gehört dieses Notebook?
2 Hotelzimmer kosten mehr während der Messe *(fair)*.
3 Ich denke über Annas Vorschlag nach. Ich denke, wir brauchen mehr Zeit.
4 Warum schaust du mich so an? – Du siehst müde aus. Ich glaube, du brauchst Urlaub.
5 Es scheint, als ob Bernd nicht kommt. Das bedeutet, dass wir anfangen können.
6 Jetzt sehe ich, dass der Preis die Transportkosten nicht einschließt.
7 Kannst du jetzt reden? – Ich esse gerade zu Mittag, aber es macht nichts.

# 5 Simple past
## Einfache Vergangenheit

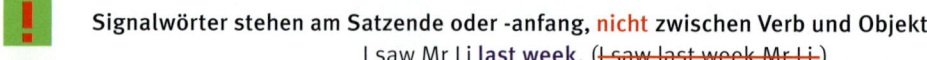

**two days ago      were           order**
This came ~~for two days~~ while you ~~was~~ away. When did you ~~ordered~~ it?

## Form

| | |
|---|---|
| ■ Verb be: was/were | I **was** new and they **were** experts. *Ich war neu und sie waren Experten.* |
| ■ Regelmäßige Verben: Infinitiv + -ed* | We **worked** hard yesterday. *Wir haben gestern hart gearbeitet.* <br> I **stayed** in a new hotel. *Ich übernachtete in einem neuen Hotel.* |
| ■ Unregelmäßige Verben: besondere Formen (s. u.) | We **took** a taxi. *Wir haben ein Taxi genommen.* <br> I **forgot** to tell you. *Ich habe vergessen, es dir zu sagen.* |
| ■ Verneinung: was/were + not sonst didn't + Infinitiv | I **wasn't** here yesterday. *Ich war gestern nicht hier.* <br> The designers **weren't** happy. *Die Designer waren nicht zufrieden.* <br> The report **didn't come** yesterday. *Der Bericht ist gestern nicht gekommen.* |
| ■ Fragen, Kurzantworten: Verb be: was/were sonst did (+ Infinitiv) | Where **was** Mr Li? *Wo war Herr Li?* <br> **Were** you here? – Yes, I **was**. / No, I **wasn't**. *Waren Sie hier? – Ja./Nein.* <br> **Did** Ed phone? – Yes, he **did**. / No, he **didn't**. *Hat Ed angerufen? – Ja./Nein.* |

\* Schreibbesonderheiten: Siehe Seite 126.

## Unregelmäßige Verben (vollständige Liste siehe Umschlagklappe)

| | | | | | | | | | |
|---|---|---|---|---|---|---|---|---|---|
| be | **was/were** | feel | **felt** | hear | **heard** | read | **read** | take | **took** |
| bring | **brought** | find | **found** | know | **knew** | ring | **rang** | tell | **told** |
| buy | **bought** | fly | **flew** | leave | **left** | run | **ran** | think | **thought** |
| come | **came** | forget | **forgot** | lose | **lost** | say | **said** | understand | **understood** |
| cost | **cost** | get | **got** | make | **made** | see | **saw** | write | **wrote** |
| do | **did** | give | **gave** | meet | **met** | sell | **sold** | | |
| drive | **drove** | go | **went** | pay | **paid** | speak | **spoke** | | |
| fall | **fell** | have | **had** | put | **put** | spend | **spent** | | |

## Gebrauch und Signalwörter

■ Mit der einfachen Vergangenheit beschreibt man abgeschlossene Ereignisse und Zustände.

■ Typische Signalwörter bezeichnen einen Zeitpunkt oder Zeitraum der abgeschlossenen Vergangenheit.

| | |
|---|---|
| **yesterday** und **last** … | yesterday, last week, last month, last year, last night, last Tuesday, last weekend |
| Ausdrücke mit **ago** | two hours ago, a few weeks ago, several months ago, ten years ago |
| **when**?, Daten | when?, (at) what time?, in 2009, on 28 December, in April |

**!** Signalwörter stehen am Satzende oder -anfang, **nicht** zwischen Verb und Objekt.
I saw Mr Li **last week**. (~~I saw last week Mr Li.~~)

**!** **ago** steht immer am Ende der Zeitbestimmung: We met two days **ago** (~~for two days~~).

## > Das Wichtigste in Kürze

■ Regelmäßige Verben: -ed; unregelmäßige Verben und be: besondere Formen
■ Frage/Verneinung mit did + Infinitiv (**nicht** did + Vergangenheitsform!)
■ Gebrauch, wenn etwas zu einem bestimmten Zeitpunkt der Vergangenheit abgeschlossen wurde

Weitere Informationen ⟶ Units 8, 9

**A** **Underline the correct form.**

1  I **didn't saw** / **didn't see** Sarah at that meeting.
2  When **bought they** / **did they buy** the firm?
3  Sales **fell** / **felt** by 10% last year.
4  This arrived **for ten minutes** / **ten minutes ago**.
5  I **stayed** / **stood** in a motel.
6  Where **was you born** / **were you born**?
7  Ed **left last year the firm** / **left the firm last year**.
8  What **did your boss** / **did your boss do**?

**B** **Make negative sentences.**

I was at the trade fair yesterday.
*I wasn't at the trade fair yesterday.*

1  I left work early yesterday.
2  This computer was expensive.
3  Sam went to China last year.
4  Judy spoke to her line manager yesterday.

**Now ask questions.**

Where / you / be yesterday?
*Where were you yesterday?*

5  What time / you / leave work yesterday?
6  How much / be / your computer?
7  Where / Sam / go last year?
8  Who / Judy / speak to yesterday?

**C** **Complete these dialogues with the verbs in the correct simple past form.**

1  A: When ................................. (the meeting / end)?

   B: Well, it ................................. (not finish) early.

2  A: ................................. (you/speak) to Martin?

   B: No, I ..................., but I ..................... (speak) to Ann.

3  A: ................................. (you/work) all weekend?

   B: No, I ................................. (not work) on Sunday.

4  A: ................................. (you/be) ill last week?

   B: Yes, I ................................. (have) the flu.

5  A: It ................................. (be) a great conference.

   B: Really? I ................................. (not think) so.

6  A: What ................................. (the licence / cost)?

   B: We ................................. (pay) $50,000.

**D** **Write questions for these answers.**

A: Where *did you grow up*?    B: I grew up in Perth.

1  A: When ........................... the company?

   B: I joined in September three years ago.

2  A: How long .................................?

   B: The presentation? It lasted 35 minutes.

3  A: ........................... Tom at the meeting?

   B: No, I didn't see him.

4  A: ..................................... everything?

   B: No, I understood very little. He spoke too fast.

**E** **Give short answers.**

1  Did they make a profit? – No, .....................
2  Did you like Shanghai? – Yes, we .................
3  Did Ed and Pete agree? – No, .....................
4  Did your boss say yes? – Yes, she .................
5  Did you enjoy your trip? – Yes, I ...................
6  Were they on time? – Yes, .........................

**F** **Translate the following sentences. Use the simple past.**

1  Ich sagte: „Wo warst du?"
2  Wir hatten ein Problem. Wir wussten nicht den Namen unseres Hotels!
3  Der Investor machte einen großen Fehler.
4  Als ich die Einladungen zur Konferenz verschickte, habe ich Eileen vergessen.

> *was working*        *were you doing*
> I ~~worked~~ on the agenda when they cancelled the meeting. What ~~did you~~?

## Form

- **was/were ...ing**     When the boss walked in, I **was imitating** him, and Ed and Max **were laughing**.
- **Verneinung**     I **wasn't running**. We **weren't hurrying**.
- **Fragen, Kurzantworten**     **Were** you **travelling**? – Yes, I **was**.
                           **Were** many people **waiting**? – No, they **weren't**.

## Gebrauch

- Mit der Verlaufsform der Vergangenheit beschreibt man etwas, das zu einem Zeitpunkt in der Vergangenheit im Verlauf begriffen, nicht abgeschlossen war, (vorübergehend) andauerte.

- **Gerade ablaufendes Geschehen**
  It **was raining** when I left the office. *Es regnete (gerade), als ich das Büro verließ.*
  At midnight we **were** still **discussing** the paper. *Um Mitternacht besprachen wir immer noch das Papier.*
  Tina was satisfied. The meeting **was going** well. *Tina war zufrieden. Die Sitzung lief gut.*

- **Vorübergehende Situation**
  I **was working** from home that week. *Ich arbeitete in der Woche von zu Hause.*

- **Längerfristige Entwicklung, die noch nicht abgeschlossen war**
  The Chinese market **was expanding**. *Der chinesische Markt expandierte.*

- **Andauernde Handlung**
  You were in the cellar for two hours. What **were** you **doing** all that time? – I **was trying** to find an old document. ... *Was hast du die ganze Zeit gemacht? – Ich habe versucht, ein altes Schriftstück zu finden.*

## Verlaufsform und einfache Form im Vergleich

- Oft benutzt man die Verlaufsform, wenn eine Situation von etwas unterbrochen wurde. Die bereits ablaufende „Hintergrund-Situation" steht in der Verlaufsform, das neue Geschehen in der einfachen Form.

       we **were driving** to the airport

I **got** a text message        now

We **were driving** to the airport when I **got** a text message from the office.
I **was standing** at reception when a colleague **walked** in.

- **Zwei nacheinander eintretende Geschehen werden beide mit der einfachen Form ausgedrückt.**
  A car **stopped** and a man **got out**.

  **Vergleiche:**     When I went in, everybody **was standing** at the window. They **were looking** out.
                    When I went in, everybody **stood up**. They all **looked** at me as if I came from Mars.

**!** Die Verlaufsform ist bei Zustandsverben normalerweise **nicht** möglich (siehe Unit 4).
When I last saw Tom he **seemed** (~~was seeming~~) very tired.

**Das Wichtigste in Kürze**
- Gebrauch: 1. vorübergehend andauernde Situation; 2. „Hintergrund-Situation", die unterbrochen wurde
- **Keine** Verlaufsform bei Zustandsverben

**A** Underline the correct form.

1 The visitors arrived when I **still prepared** / **was still preparing** the conference room.

2 **Did anyone wait** / **Was anyone waiting** for you when you got back to the hotel?

3 I tried to call you at six. **What did you do?** / **What were you doing?**

4 When I first joined the company, I **didn't want** / **wasn't wanting** a company car.

5 Arthur **fell** / **was falling** down the stairs last week and **broke** / **was breaking** his leg.

6 I **didn't see** / **wasn't seeing** the other car. I **thought** / **was thinking** about a problem I had at work.

**B** Make questions and answers.

What / you / do / when the news / come through from Beijing? – I / sit in a meeting.

*What were you doing when the news came through from Beijing? – I was sitting in a meeting.*

1 What sort of work / Tony / do / when they / move him to marketing? – He / work in HR.

2 When the accident / happen, how fast / they / drive? – They / travel at over 100 km an hour.

3 Who / John / speak to / when the secretary / walk in? – He / phone his girlfriend.

4 When / the CEO / become ill, / which country / he / visit? – He / attend a conference in Singapore.

5 Where / the two presenters / stand / when the screen / fall down? – They / just set up the computer.

**C** Complete these dialogues with the verbs in the simple past or the past progressive.

A: Guess who I **saw** (see) when I **was waiting** (wait) in the departure lounge.

B: No idea. Jamie Oliver?

1 A: ............................. (it/snow) when you ............................. (get) to Denver?

B: Yes, but when I ......................... (get up) the next day the sun ......................... (shine).

2 A: Why ............................. (you/switch) the photocopier off?

B: Nobody ....................... (use) it and I ......................... (want) to save electricity.

3 A: ............................. (you/phone) the Texas office yesterday?

B: No, I'm afraid I ........................... (forget). I ............................. (remember) when

I ..................... (come) out of the marketing meeting, but then it ................. (be) too late.

4 A: Where ......................... (you/go) when I ........................... (see) you yesterday

afternoon? You ......................... (seem) to be in a hurry.

B: I was. I ......................... (go) to court. That's why I ........................... (wear) that

dark suit.

5 A: The presenter ........................... (give) us some information about cultural differences.

B: Did she? I ..................... (miss) that part of the talk because I ........................... (go)

to sort out a problem in the production department. When I ......................... (come) back, she

......................... (talk) about prices.

**D** Translate the following sentences.

1 Als mein Kollege ins Zimmer kam, testeten wir gerade eine Simulation auf dem Computer.

2 Ich habe Sie angerufen. Wo waren Sie? – Ich saß in der U-Bahn und habe mein Handy nicht gehört.

3 Haben Sie Marina gestern gesehen? – Ja, sie sah furchtbar aus. Sie hatte eine schlimme Erkältung.

4 Als wir in London ankamen, regnete es. Wir wollten nach Barcelona zurückfliegen.

5 Letzte Woche um diese Zeit saß ich in einem Büro in Kuala Lumpur.

# 7 Present perfect
## Present Perfect

> **have missed   recently**
> Where's Jo? I ~~missed~~ her ~~in the last time~~.

> **has gone**
> She ~~is gone~~ to Korea. She's there for three months.

## Form

- **have** oder **has** +
  **Partizip Perfekt**

  The business **has moved**. They**'ve bought** office space in the new Rymex Centre.
  *Die Firma ist umgezogen. Sie haben Büroräume im neuen Rymex-Center gekauft.*

- **Form des Partizips:**
  regelmäßige Verben*:
  wie Vergangenheitsform
  unregelmäßige Verben:
  besondere Formen (s.u.)

  I**'ve booked** a table for 7 p.m.  *Ich habe einen Tisch für 19 Uhr reserviert.*
  My visa for Vietnam **has arrived**.  *Mein Visum für Vietnam ist gekommen.*
  The Koreans **have sent** some questions.  *Die Koreaner haben einige Fragen geschickt.*
  The price **has fallen**.  *Der Preis ist gefallen.*

- **Verneinung: have/has**
  **+ not**

  I **haven't asked** Mr Li yet. There **hasn't been** an opportunity.
  *Ich habe Herrn Li noch nicht gefragt. Es gab noch keine Gelegenheit.*

- **Fragen, Kurzantworten:**
  **have/has**

  **Have** you **eaten**? – Yes, I **have**. / No, I **haven't**.  *Haben Sie gegessen? – Ja./Nein.*
  **Has** Ed **come**? – Yes, he **has**. / No, he **hasn't**.  *Ist Ed gekommen? – Ja./Nein.*

*Schreibbesonderheiten: Siehe Seite 126.

## Unregelmäßige Verben (vollständige Liste siehe Umschlagklappe)

| | | | | | | | | |
|---|---|---|---|---|---|---|---|---|
| be | was/were | **been** | get | got | **got / gotten** | read | read | **read** |
| bring | brought | **brought** | give | gave | **given** | say | said | **said** |
| buy | bought | **bought** | go | went | **gone** | see | saw | **seen** |
| come | came | **come** | have | had | **had** | speak | spoke | **spoken** |
| cost | cost | **cost** | hear | heard | **heard** | spend | spent | **spent** |
| do | did | **done** | know | knew | **known** | take | took | **taken** |
| fall | fell | **fallen** | leave | left | **left** | tell | told | **told** |
| feel | felt | **felt** | make | made | **made** | think | thought | **thought** |
| find | found | **found** | meet | met | **met** | understand | understood | **understood** |
| forget | forgot | **forgotten** | pay | paid | **paid** | write | wrote | **written** |

## Gebrauch und Signalwörter

Mit dem Present Perfect wird ausgedrückt, dass etwas – irgendwann – in der Zeit bis jetzt geschehen ist.
Der Zeitpunkt ist entweder unwichtig oder unbekannt; im Vordergrund steht allein die Tatsache, **dass** etwas
geschehen ist. Wird der Zeitpunkt genannt, darf das Present Perfect nicht gebraucht werden (siehe Units 8, 9).

- **Typische Signalwörter sind Ausdrücke für die ganze Zeit bis jetzt sowie für die (aller)letzte Zeit.**
  die ganze Zeit bis jetzt   already *(schon)*, yet? *(schon – in Fragen)*, before *(schon einmal)*, so far *(bisher)*
  always *(schon immer)*, ever? *(je? schon einmal?)*, never *(nie)*, not yet *(noch nicht)*
  die (aller)letzte Zeit   just *(gerade)*, recently *(in letzter Zeit)*, lately *(in letzter Zeit)*

- **Stellung: so far, before, yet, recently, lately** stehen am Satzende, andere Ausdrücke vor dem Partizip.
  I**'ve met** Mr Li **before**, but I **haven't met** Shuna **yet**.   I**'ve never been** to Saigon. **Have** you **ever been** there?

> ## Das Wichtigste in Kürze
> - Regelmäßige Verben: have/has + -ed; unregelmäßige Verben: besondere Formen
> - Das Present Perfect ist **nicht** möglich, wenn ein bestimmter Zeitpunkt genannt wird

Weitere Informationen ⟶ Units 8–10

**A** **Underline the correct form.**

1 I've chosen / I've chose Jemma to represent us.
2 We haven't made a decision already / yet.
3 Have you ever been to / Were you already in Moscow?
4 I have before visited Singapore. / I have visited Singapore before.
5 I'm sorry, Ms Smart has gone / is gone to the airport to meet a client.
6 Max has had a lot of stress in the last time / lately.

**B** **Make complete sentences with the present perfect.**

(never) I / be / Canada  I've never been to Canada.

1 (always) we / buy from a French company
2 (ever) your boss / fall asleep in a meeting?
3 (just) I / finish the system check
4 (yet) you / do your project description?
5 (before) Paul / be / the USA
6 (recently) I / have a lot of work

**C** **Complete these dialogues with the correct form of the present perfect.**

1 A: What's the matter with Tom?  B: He ............................. (just hear) some bad news.

2 A: What's the new bistro like?  B: I don't know. I ............................. (try) it yet.

3 A: Are Ed and Max still here or ............................. (they/go) to lunch?

  B: I'm afraid you ............................. (just miss) them. They ............................. (just leave).

4 A: ............................. (your colleague / change) his attitude?

  B: No, even though he ............................. (have) lots of complaints.

**D** **Give short answers.**

Have you booked a table? – Yes, I have.

1 Has Craig sent out those documents? –

  No, .............................

2 Have you heard from Mexico? –

  Yes, .............................

3 Have the cleaners been in yet? –

  No, .............................

4 Has Jonathan Stokes phoned? –

  Yes, .............................

**E** **Write questions for these answers.**

A: Have you ever been to any of the Gulf states?
B: The Gulf states? No, I haven't, and I don't really want to.

1 A: How many people .............................?

  B: I've invited twenty.

2 A: How many applications .......................?

  B: John? He's written hundreds.

3 A: ............................. to Shanghai?

  B: Yes, we have – it's a great city.

4 A: Ann, this is Mr Sharma.

  ............................. before?

  B: Yes, we have. We met last year in Bombay.

**F** **Translate the following sentences.**

1 Wir haben in letzter Zeit viele Probleme gehabt.
2 Waren Sie schon mal in einer Karaoke-Bar in Japan?
3 Ich habe schon immer ein Büro ohne Telefon und Computer haben wollen!
4 Haben Sie es vergessen? Die Japaner kommen heute.
5 Ist unser Geld gekommen? Haben sie unsere Rechnung bezahlt?
6 Ich habe die Präsentation [schon] so oft gehört.

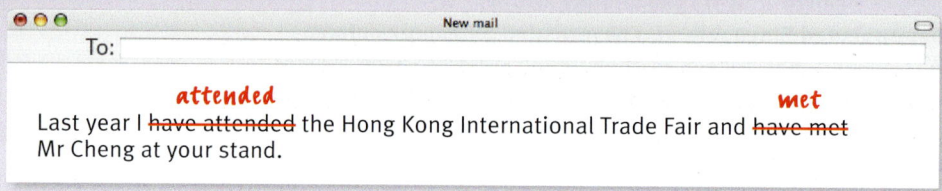

> **attended**      **met**
> Last year I ~~have attended~~ the Hong Kong International Trade Fair and ~~have met~~ Mr Cheng at your stand.

### Present Perfect

- Mit dem Present Perfect wird ausgedrückt, dass etwas irgendwann in der Zeit bis zur Gegenwart geschehen ist.

  I **have been** to the USA. ⋯⟩
  Martin **has visited** the factory in Korea. ⋯⟩

- Fragen werden gestellt, um zu erfahren, ob etwas überhaupt (d. h. in der ganzen Zeit bis jetzt) geschehen ist.

  **Have** you ever **been** to Mumbai? – Yes, I have. ⋯⟩
  **Has** Tom **phoned**? – Yes, he has. ⋯⟩

### Einfache Vergangenheit

- Mit der einfachen Vergangenheit wird ausgedrückt, dass etwas zu einem bestimmten Zeitpunkt in der Vergangenheit abgeschlossen wurde.
  I **went** there last year.
  He **visited** it two months ago.

- Fragen werden gestellt, um zu erfahren, wann (d. h. zu welchem vergangenen Zeitpunkt) etwas geschehen ist.
  When **did** you **go** there?
  When **did** he **ring**?

### Gegenwartsbezug des Present Perfect

- Mit dem Present Perfect wird über etwas gesprochen, das jetzt in der Gegenwart Auswirkungen hat (deshalb auch der Name <u>Present</u> Perfect).
  I**'ve been** to Alaska. [= Ich kenne Alaska.]
  I **have read** the report on corruption. [= Ich bin jetzt informiert.]
  They**'ve changed** the password. [= Wir brauchen das neue, um uns einloggen zu können.]

### Present Perfect und einfache Vergangenheit mit und ohne Zeitangaben

- Beide Zeitformen werden mit typischen Signalwörtern gebraucht (siehe Units 5, 7). Wird ein Zeitpunkt oder abgeschlossener Zeitraum in der Vergangenheit genannt, so muss man die einfache Vergangenheit verwenden.

  I **have had** this sort of problem once **before**. ⋯⟩   It **happened** sometime **in the summer**.
  Sonia **has given** this presentation **many times**. ⋯⟩   **The last time was** at that conference **in February**.

- Auch wenn kein Zeitpunkt genannt wird, muss die einfache Vergangenheit gebraucht werden, wenn sich das Geschehen zu einem ganz bestimmten Zeitpunkt in der Vergangenheit ereignet haben muss.
  Mrs Snowdon's grandfather **founded** the company. [= Als er damals lebte.]

  Vergleiche:
  Ann **has found** a mobile phone. [= Sie hat es jetzt.]
  Someone **left** it in the canteen. [= Es wurde zu einem bestimmten Zeitpunkt dort liegen gelassen.]

  Max **has worked** in lots of different countries. [= Er hat Auslandserfahrung.]
  He **spent** over two years in India. [= Sein Aufenthalt wurde in der Vergangenheit beendet, er ist nicht mehr dort.]

  John **has broken** his arm. [= Er ist verletzt.]
  He **fell** on some ice in the car park. [= Der Unfall ereignete sich dort, ist aber jetzt vorbei.]

  We**'ve bought** a new printer. [= Wir haben jetzt einen neuen.]
  How much **did** you **pay** for it? [= Wie teuer war er zum Zeitpunkt der Bezahlung?]

### Das Wichtigste in Kürze

- Present Perfect: Etwas hat sich irgendwann ereignet und hat jetzt Auswirkungen, ist jetzt relevant
- Nur einfache Vergangenheit möglich, wenn ein bestimmter Zeitpunkt genannt oder gedacht wird!

Weitere Informationen → Units 7, 9, 10

**A** **Underline the correct form.**

1 The economic crisis **broke out** / **has broken out** in the autumn of 2008.
2 Interest rates **have risen** / **rose** again. They are at an all-time high.
3 I **had** / **have had** a nice surprise two days ago.
4 We **didn't have** / **haven't had** time to discuss everything at yesterday's meeting.
5 When **did you receive** / **have you received** this message?
6 Diana is an expert. She **had** / **has had** a lot of experience in that field. Ask her.

**B** **Make dialogues as in the example.**

A: you / ever / **work** in the USA? *Have you ever worked in the USA?*
B: Yes, I / **work** there for six months in 2009. *Yes, I worked there for six months in 2009.*

1 A: you / **find** a hotel yet?
   B: Yes, I / **check into** one ten minutes ago.

2 A: you / **read** the report?
   B: I / **have a look** at it this morning.

3 A: you / ever / **travel** on the train to Tibet?
   B: Yes, I / **take** it just after the line opened.

4 A: you / **complete** your preparation yet?
   B: Yes, I / **do** it yesterday.

**C** **Complete these dialogues with the verbs in the present perfect, where it is possible, and the simple past where it is not.**

A: I **went** (go) to the Nigerian stand yesterday. **Have you visited** (you/visit) it yet?
B: No, I **wanted** (want) to go an hour ago, but there **were** (be) so many potential clients here, I couldn't get away.

1 A: Do you have any more news? ........................... (you/speak) to Dave?

   B: No. I ........................... (phone) his office at 2 o'clock and I ........................... (call)

   again at 2.30, but he ........................... (still not be) back from lunch.

2 A: ........................... (you/learn) French when you were at school?

   B: Yes, but that ........................... (be) 20 years ago and now I ...........................

   (forget) most of it. I ........................... (not like) the French teacher and so I

   ........................... (never do) any work.

3 A: We ........................... (not decide) if we're going away for the weekend. What about you?

   B: Well, Ray ........................... (say) an hour ago that someone has to be in the office on

   Saturday. I don't think he ........................... (decide) who will have to come in.

4 A: Last week I ........................... (buy) a new-generation smartphone. I ...........................

   (never have) one with so many applications before.

   B: When I ........................... (be) younger I ........................... (be) a real gadget freak,

   I ........................... (always want) the very latest model, but now I'm not really bothered any

   more. It's at least four years since I last ........................... (buy) a new phone.

**D** **Translate the following sentences. Use the present perfect, where it is possible, and the simple past where it is not.**

1 Ed hat ein neues Notebook gekauft. Er hat vor zwei Tagen ein günstiges [= billiges] Angebot gefunden.
2 Willst du dieses Buch? Ich habe es zu Ende gelesen *(finish)*. Ich habe es auf dem Rückflug gelesen.
3 Haben Sie die Einladungen geschrieben? – Nein, gestern hatte ich keine Zeit.
4 Hat Ronaldo Ihnen alle Dokumente gegeben? – Nein. Er hat sie mir [schon] letzte Woche versprochen, aber ich habe bisher nichts bekommen. Ich habe ihn vor zwei Stunden [daran] erinnert *(remind)*.
5 Haben Sie von Ann gehört? – Ja, sie ist angekommen. Sie hat vor zehn Minuten eine SMS geschickt.

> I had
> ~~I've had~~ a terrible morning today, but the afternoon has been better.

### Present Perfect und einfache Vergangenheit mit den gleichen Zeitangaben

In den Units 5 und 7 wurden Zeitangaben genannt, die für die Verwendung des Present Perfect oder der einfachen Vergangenheit typisch sind. Manche kann man jedoch mit beiden Zeitformen verwenden.

- **just** wird ohne Bedeutungsunterschied mit beiden Zeitformen gebraucht.
  I've just spoken / I just spoke to Ellen. *Ich habe gerade mit Ellen gesprochen.*

- **already** *(schon)*, **not yet** *(noch nicht)*, **yet?** *(schon?)*, **so far** *(bisher)* verwendet man mit dem Present Perfect, wenn die Bedeutung „in der ganzen Zeit bis jetzt" entspricht.
  Besonders im amerikanischen Englisch ist jedoch auch die einfache Vergangenheit möglich.
  I've already informed / I already informed head office. *Ich habe die Hauptverwaltung bereits informiert.*
  The sample hasn't arrived yet / didn't arrive yet. *Das Muster ist noch nicht angekommen.*
  Has Frank called back yet? / Did Frank call back yet? *Hat Frank schon zurückgerufen?*
  The work has been easy so far / The work was easy so far. *Die Arbeit war bisher leicht.*

- Das Gleiche gilt für **always**, **ever** und **never** in der Bedeutung „in der ganzen Zeit bis jetzt".
  I have always kept / always kept a copy of important documents. *Ich habe immer eine Kopie … behalten.*
  Have you ever travelled / Did you ever travel on Eurostar? *Sind Sie schon jemals mit dem Eurostar gereist?*
  I've never seen / I never saw such chaos. *Ich habe noch nie ein solches Chaos gesehen.*

**!** Wenn aber ein Zeitraum gemeint ist, der zu einem bestimmten Zeitpunkt der Vergangenheit zu Ende ging („damals schon", „damals noch nicht" usw.), verwendet man nur die einfache Vergangenheit.
When I informed my boss she already knew. *Als ich meine Chefin informierte, wusste sie schon Bescheid.*
In the days before computers people always kept copies. *In der Zeit … hat man immer Kopien behalten.*
Under the old management there was never chaos. *Unter der alten Firmenleitung gab es nie Chaos.*

**!** Auch Zeitangaben mit **this …** und **today** können mit dem Present Perfect oder der einfachen Vergangenheit gebraucht werden. Ist der Zeitraum abgeschlossen, muss die einfache Vergangenheit verwendet werden.
*(morgens, 11 Uhr)* I've had three cappuccinos this morning. *Ich habe heute Morgen [bisher] … getrunken.*
*(ab Mittag)* I had three cappuccinos this morning. *Ich trank heute Morgen drei Cappuccino.*

| Present Perfect | Einfache Vergangenheit |
|---|---|
| ■ Das Present Perfect ist möglich, wenn über die ganze Zeit bis hin zur Gegenwart gesprochen wird; wenn etwas irgendwann in dieser Zeit geschehen ist.<br>We've sold 10,000 so far.<br>This year has brought some restructuring. | ■ Die einfache Vergangenheit muss verwendet werden, wenn etwas zu einem bestimmten Zeitpunkt oder in einem abgeschlossenen Zeitraum in der Vergangenheit geschah und beendet wurde.<br>We sold 4,000 last year.<br>They brought in new management some time ago. |
| ■ Die Handlung oder Situation ist noch relevant und hat noch Auswirkungen in der Gegenwart.<br>It's been a difficult week. I'm feeling very tired.<br>We've done business with him before. He's reliable. | ■ Die Handlung oder Situation ist abgeschlossen und gehört der Vergangenheit an.<br>Last week was even worse.<br>We first did business with him in 2008. |

**>** **Das Wichtigste in Kürze**
- Present Perfect: irgendwann in der Zeit bis jetzt geschehen und jetzt noch relevant und aktuell
- Einfache Vergangenheit: in der Vergangenheit abgeschlossen, beendet

**A** **Underline the correct form. Underline both forms if both are correct.**

1  The Chinese delegation  **has just arrived**  /  **just arrived**.
2  Mo Walker left the company before I  **have joined**  /  **joined**.
3  When I worked in Australia, I  **always spent**  /  **have always spent**  Christmas Day on the beach.
4  That legendary Model T Ford – how many of them  **did Henry Ford build**  /  **has Henry Ford built**?
5  There has been no 4 p.m. bulletin because this morning's meeting  **didn't take place**  /  **hasn't taken place**.
6  At university they  **have never prepared**  /  **never prepared**  me for the stress that I have in my job.

**B** **Use the present perfect, where it is possible.**

*(It's 6 p.m.)* I **didn't have** (not have) breakfast today.

1  *(It's June.)* I .............................. (not have) a single day off this year yet.

2  *(It's 11 a.m.)* My alarm clock ............................. (not ring) this morning and I was late.

3  *(It's September.)* We ............................. (not have) a very successful year so far.

4  *(It's Thursday.)* Harry, why ........................... (you/be) late for work every morning this week?

5  *(It's Sunday evening.)* I ........................... (not think) about the office once this weekend!

**C** **Complete these dialogues with the verbs in the present perfect or simple past.**

1  A: It's 11 o'clock and I still .......................... (not finish) this afternoon's presentation!

   I ......................... (do) an outline when I .......................... (come in) first thing this

   morning – but that's all.

   B: Can I help at all? I ......................... (finish) my report ten minutes ago, so I have a bit of time.

2  A: What a week! I ......................... (work) all day yesterday without a break and

   I ......................... (not have) a break today either. I'm glad there's only one more hour to go!

   B: I ......................... (get) some sandwiches from the canteen at lunchtime – would you like one?

3  A: Jason told me about your notebook. How .......................... (you/lose) it?

   B: Well, I ......................... (have) it with me in the conference room this morning and then

   I ......................... (leave) it there when we ......................... (break) for lunch, but someone

   ......................... (forget) to lock the room and after lunch it ......................... (be) gone.

4  A: I ......................... (decide) to go to the Indian international trade fair this year – it's next

   month. ......................................... (you / ever attend) it?

   B: Yes, a couple of years ago. My old boss .......................... (send) me. It really

   ......................... (be) very interesting. I .......................... (learn) a lot.

**D** **Translate the following sentences.**

1  Ich bin im Urlaub. Es ist 15.00 Uhr und ich habe den ganzen Tag nichts getan. Gestern habe ich den ganzen Tag am Pool gelegen. Fantastisch!

2  Vor zehn Jahren habe ich Kenia als Tourist besucht und letzte Woche erfuhr [hörte] ich, dass ich das Büro dort übernehme.

3  Als Kollegin war Maria immer freundlich und hilfsbereit. Es ist schade, dass sie die Firma Ende letzten Jahres verlassen hat.

4  Es ist schon Donnerstag und wir haben nichts gehört. Am Dienstag haben sie eine Antwort innerhalb von 24 Stunden versprochen.

# 10 Present perfect with expressions like *since* and *for*
## Present Perfect mit Ausdrücken wie *since* und *for*

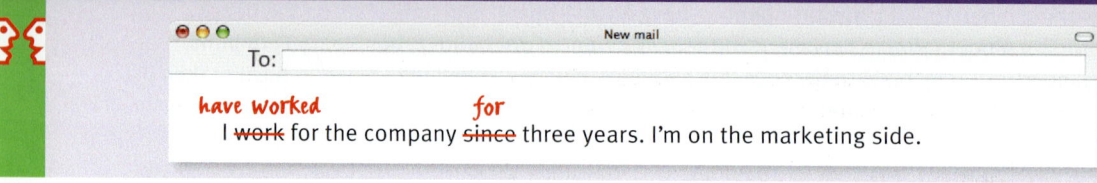

have worked          for

I ~~work~~ for the company ~~since~~ three years. I'm on the marketing side.

**!** **Present Perfect für nicht abgeschlossene Zustände**

Bis in die Gegenwart andauernde Zustände werden mit dem Present Perfect ausgedrückt: Etwas hat in der Vergangenheit begonnen und dauert bis jetzt an. Im Deutschen wird in solchen Fällen meist die Gegenwart gebraucht.

The firm is in difficulties. I**'ve known** this a long time. ... *Ich weiß es schon lange.*

**Gebrauch mit typischen Zeitangaben**

■ Bis in die Gegenwart andauernde Zustände werden mit Zeitangaben wie always, all ..., a long time sowie mit since und for (beide „seit") ausgedrückt.

It**'s always been** a pleasure to do business with you. *Es war schon immer eine Freude, ...*
We need more people in this team. I**'ve thought** this **all along**. ... *Das denke ich schon die ganze Zeit.*
There **have been** problems with the intranet **all week**. *Es gibt schon die ganze Woche Probleme mit ...*
I**'ve known** Mark **a long time**. *Ich kenne Mark schon lange.*
Rob **has had** a new assistant **since** last month. *Rob hat seit letztem Monat einen neuen Assistenten.*
Mr Schmidt **has worked** here **for** 26 years. *Herr Schmidt arbeitet seit 26 Jahren hier.*

■ Mit since benennt man den Anfangszeitpunkt, an dem etwas begonnen hat.

since = „seit" + Zeitpunkt
since 1999, **since** 4 o'clock, **since** yesterday, **since** Tuesday, **since** last year

There**'s been** (~~There's~~) a problem **since** Monday.
*Es gibt seit Montag ein Problem.*
We**'ve known** (~~We know~~) Mr Li **since** 2000.
*Wir kennen Herrn Li seit 2000.*
I**'ve been** (~~I am~~) here **since** 9 o'clock.
*Ich bin seit 9 Uhr hier.*

■ Mit for nennt man eine Zeitspanne und sagt, wie lange etwas andauert.

for = „seit" + Zeitspanne
for five minutes, **for** two hours, **for** six weeks, **for** a month, **for** years, **for** ages *(seit Ewigkeiten)*

There**'s been** (~~There's~~) a problem **for** two days now.
*Es gibt jetzt seit zwei Tagen ein Problem.*
We**'ve known** (~~We know~~) Mr Li **for** over ten years.
*Wir kennen Herrn Li seit über zehn Jahren.*
It's 11 now, so I**'ve been** (~~I am~~) here **for** two hours.
*Es ist jetzt 11, also bin ich seit zwei Stunden hier.*

■ Auch in Fragen mit How long? wird das Present Perfect gebraucht, wenn ein Zeitraum bis zur Gegenwart gemeint ist.

**How long have** you **been** in Berlin? *Seit wann / Wie lange sind Sie (schon) in Berlin?*
**How long have** you **known** each other? *Wie lange kennen Sie sich (schon)?*

**!** Wenn mit since, for, how long, all ... ein abgeschlossener Zeitraum in der Vergangenheit gemeint ist, muss das Verb in der einfachen Vergangenheit stehen.

Andy is ill. He **has had** the flu **for** two weeks.
I**'ve been** in this department **for** three years.
**How long have** you **worked** here?
It**'s been** cold **all** week.

Tim is fit again. He **was** ill **for** two weeks.
Before that I **was** in sales **for** three years.
**How long did** you **work** in your old firm?
It **was** cold **all** last week.

**>** **Das Wichtigste in Kürze**

■ Present Perfect bei Zuständen, die bis in die Gegenwart andauern
■ „seit" = since + Zeitpunkt, for + Zeitspanne

Weitere Informationen ⟶ Units 7–9

**A** **Underline the correct form.**

1 How long **do you know** / **have you known** Hermione?

2 The consultant has been here **since two weeks** / **for two weeks**.

3 Ms Garston **has been** / **was** in Beijing all last week.

4 The boss **has been** / **was** in Mr Keller's office a long time before she came to us.

5 The documents **are** / **have been** in the cellar **since** / **for** ages.

6 Prices exploded and **have remained** / **remain** high ever since.

**B** **Complete the sentences with the present perfect and since or for.**

1 We ......................... (know) each other ............ ages.

2 Angela ......................... (be) in Munich ............ last week.

3 I ......................... (not feel) well ............ I got up.

4 He......................... (not have) a day off ............ weeks.

**C** **Complete these dialogues with the verbs in the correct form and choose since or for.**

1 A: ......................... (you/meet) Piotr before?

   B: Yes, we ......................... (know) each other **since/for** we were colleagues in Warsaw.

2 A: How long ......................... (your boss / be) off work sick?

   B: **Since/For** sometime in June. He ................... (have) a heart attack while away on a business trip.

3 A: I ......................... (not see) Barry Ogilvie **since/for** that meeting we .........................

   (have) in the Walton Hotel. ......................... (you/have) any contact recently?

   B: He ......................... (be) away twice at the beginning of the month, but ..................... (be)

   back **since/for** several days, although I ......................... (not speak) to him **since/for** his return.

4 A: How long ......................... (you/be) with this company?

   B: **Since/For** I left university. I ......................... (never have) another job.

**D** **Complete this email with the correct form of the verbs.**

You ......................[1] **(want)** me to find out who ......................[2] **(be)** team secretary in the S.E.

Asia department when we ......................[3] **(sign)** the contract with Kafmai Industries back in 2001.

Well, as you know, there ......................[4] **(not be)** a S.E. Asia department since 2007, but last week I

......................[5] **(request)** a list from HR of all the people who ......................[6] **(work)** in the

department before we ......................[7] **(set up)** the separate sales units for Mainland China, Hong

Kong and Taiwan in that year. I ......................[8] **(check)** through the list, but all the people involved

in the Kafmai project ......................[9] **(now leave)** the company. Alice Dougan is our longest-serving

member of staff – she ......................[10] **(be)** with the company for over 20 years – but she

......................[11] **(not know)** the secretary's name when I ......................[12] **(ask)** her.

**E** **Translate the following sentences.**

1 Ich bin seit einer Woche hier in Samara und habe einige interessante Leute kennen gelernt.

2 Wir haben schon den ganzen Tag Probleme mit dem Computersystem.

3 Wie viele Tage ist Frau Adam [schon] in Riga? Wann ist sie angekommen?

4 Wie lange kennen Sie Shuna? – Wir kennen uns schon lange, aber wir sind erst seit Mai Kolleginnen.

**have been writing for**
I ~~write~~ emails ~~since~~ an hour. I still haven't finished.

**have been answering    answered**
And I ~~answer~~ emails. I've ~~been answering~~ forty so far.

## Form

- have/has been …ing        I've **been preparing** the conference. Sue **has been helping** me.
- haven't/hasn't been …ing  We **haven't been flirting**.
- have/has been …ing?       **Have** you **been spying** on us? – No, I **haven't**.

## Gebrauch

- Die Verlaufsform des Present Perfect drückt aus, dass eine Handlung oder ein Vorgang in der Vergangenheit begonnen hat und (ggfs. mit Unterbrechungen) bis in die Gegenwart andauert oder vor kurzem zu Ende ging.
  We **have been sitting** (~~We are sitting~~) here since 9 o'clock.  *Wir sitzen hier seit 9 Uhr.*
  Max **has been travelling** (~~Max travels~~) a lot recently.  *Max reist viel in letzter Zeit.*
  I've **been phoning** (~~I phone~~) customers all day, but that was the last and now I'm going home.  *Ich telefoniere schon den ganzen Tag mit Kunden, aber dieser war der letzte und jetzt gehe ich nach Hause.*

Die Verlaufsform ist **nicht** möglich bei Zustandsverben wie **know**, **have** usw. (siehe Liste Unit 4). Bei diesen Verben werden bis in die Gegenwart andauernde Zustände mit der einfachen Form des Present Perfect ausgedrückt (siehe Unit 10).
~~I have been knowing Janet for 10 years~~. I **have known** Janet for 10 years.  *Ich kenne Janet seit 10 Jahren.*
~~I have been having a cold since Monday~~. I **have had** a cold since Monday.  *Ich bin seit Montag erkältet.*

## Gebrauchsunterschied zwischen Verlaufsform und einfacher Form des Present Perfect

- Bei bestimmten Verben (z. B. **live**, **work**) kann man beide Formen ohne Unterschied gebrauchen.
  I **have been living** here for a long time. / I **have lived** here for a long time.  *Ich wohne schon lange hier.*
  Ed **has been working** for us since 2007. / Ed **has worked** for us since 2007.  *Ed arbeitet seit 2007 bei uns.*

- Die Verlaufsform betont die Handlung und deren Andauern, die einfache Form drückt das Endergebnis aus (oft Antwort auf die Frage „wie viel/viele").
  I've **been interviewing** candidates all day.        I've **interviewed** 15 candidates.
  You look tired. – I've **been reading** reports.        I've **read** six long reports.
  How long **have** you **been trying** to reach me?        I've **tried** at least eight times.
  I've **been doing** the budget. My head is full of numbers.        I've **checked** everything and it all looks OK.

## > Das Wichtigste in Kürze

- Verlaufsform des Present Perfect, wenn etwas bis jetzt andauert
- Zustände: nur einfache Form (**nicht** Verlaufsform) des Present Perfect
- Bei Handlungen/Vorgängen: Verlaufsform betont Handlung und Andauern; einfache Form betont Endergebnis

**A** **Underline the correct form.**

1 I **have been working** / **work** for this company since 2008.

2 Max **has been doing** / **has done** over 30 hours overtime this month.

3 Sorry for the delay. **Are you waiting** / **Have you been waiting** long?

4 We **have been knowing** / **have known** each other for a long time.

5 How much **have we been spending** / **have we spent** so far on consultants this year?

6 Where have you been? – **I've been studying** / **I've studied** the plans for the new building.

**B** **Present perfect or present perfect progressive?**

1 I ............................. (work) for four different IT companies so far.

I ............................. (be) at this one since last year.

2 How long ............................. (Jake/learn) to use the new system?

How many sessions ............................. (he/have) with the IT specialist so far?

3 Janet ............................. (talk) to the Japanese office on Skype® for 45 minutes now.

She ............................. (make) six long calls since she got back from lunch.

4 Ed's stressed out because he ............................. (set up) a new operation in Indonesia.

He's almost finished. He ............................. (make) several visits to Kuala Lumpur.

**C** **Complete these sentences with the verbs in the correct form: present progressive, present perfect or present perfect progressive.**

1 (build) They ............................. two new warehouses at the moment.

They ............................. them since last year.

They ............................. a new access road, too. They did that first.

2 (check) I ............................. the new catalogue texts all afternoon.

I ............................. the section on export products at the moment.

I'm almost through. I ............................. at least 80% of the texts now.

**D** **Complete these dialogues with the verbs in the correct form: simple present, present perfect or present perfect progressive.**

1 A: How long ............................. (you / look for) a new job?

B: I ............................. (try) to find one since May. I .............................

(know) since then that my job will probably be lost in the restructuring.

2 A: Where ............................. (you/be)? I ............................. (not see) you all afternoon.

B: I ............................. (discuss) next year's budget with my colleagues the whole time.

3 A: Congratulations on your new job! How ............................. (you/like) it?

B: I ............................. (only be) there for a few days, but it ............................. (seem) fine.

**E** **Translate the following sentences.**

1 Wir wohnen nicht mehr in einem Hotel. Wir haben seit drei Wochen eine Wohnung in Taipei City.

2 Kennen Sie Mr Li? – Ja, wir kennen uns seit mehreren Jahren.

3 Ich habe gerade Probleme mit einer Kollegin. Wir sprechen seit drei Tagen nicht mehr miteinander.

4 Ich arbeite in der Exportabteilung. Wie lange arbeiten Sie schon hier?

5 Jackie arbeitet schon immer viel, aber in der letzten Zeit arbeitet sie zu viel.

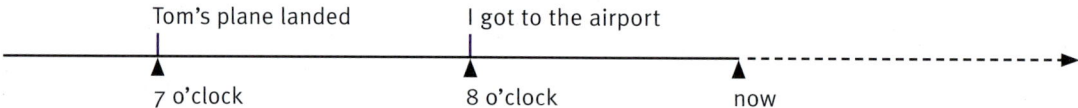

When I arrived, they ~~already discussed~~ **had already discussed** several items on the agenda. They ~~were waiting~~ **had been waiting** for me for over two hours.

## Form

- **Einfache Form: had(n't)**
  **+ Partizip Perfekt**

  I arrived at 9.00. By 10.30 I **had seen** five people, but I **hadn't met** Mr Li.
  **Had** you **spoken** to Wang? – Yes, I **had**. / No, I **hadn't**.

- **Verlaufsform: had(n't)**
  **been ...ing**

  Ed came in. I **had(n't) been expecting** him.
  **Had** you **been expecting** anyone? – Yes, I **had**. / No, I **hadn't**.

## Gebrauch

- Mit dem Past Perfect wird gesagt, dass etwas vor einem Zeitpunkt in der Vergangenheit abgeschlossen wurde.

| Tom's plane landed | I got to the airport | |
|---|---|---|
| ▲ | ▲ | ▲ - - - - - - - - ▶ |
| 7 o'clock | 8 o'clock | now |

When I got to the airport, Tom's plane **had** already **landed**.

- Die Verlaufsform des Past Perfect drückt aus, dass etwas vor einem vergangenen Zeitpunkt angefangen hatte und bis zu diesem Zeitpunkt andauerte. Die Dauer wird oft mit for oder since angegeben.
  He **had been waiting for** a whole hour / **since** 7 o'clock. *Er wartete schon eine ganze Stunde / seit 7 Uhr.*

 Bei Zustandsverben ist die Verlaufsform **nicht** möglich (siehe Liste Unit 4).
I **hadn't known** (~~hadn't been knowing~~) that he would take an earlier flight.

## Gebrauchsunterschiede

- Die Verlaufsform betont die Handlung und deren Andauern, die einfache Form drückt das Endergebnis aus. Die Verlaufsform ist meist nicht möglich, wenn ein Ergebnis (Frage „wie viel/viele") genannt wird
  He **had been looking** round the airport shops.          He **had bought** a book and two magazines.

- Wenn zwei Handlungen hintereinander geschehen und die zweite eine logische Folge oder Reaktion der ersten darstellt, werden beide mit der einfachen Vergangenheit ausgedrückt.
  Kim **introduced** herself and then **started** her presentation.

  Soll aber ausgedrückt werden, dass die erste vorher abgeschlossen wurde, steht diese im Past Perfect.
  She **had said** at the beginning that it would last 40 minutes, but people **started** to leave after half an hour.

- In Nebensätzen mit as soon as, after, before, until kann das Past Perfect ODER die einfache Vergangenheit stehen.
  **As soon as** / **After** we **(had) left** the airport, it started raining.
  It didn't stop **before/until** we **(had) got** to the office.

 **Das Wichtigste in Kürze**
- Past Perfect, wenn etwas vor einem Zeitpunkt in der Vergangenheit abgeschlossen wurde
- Verlaufsform betont Andauern von etwas bis zu einem Zeitpunkt in der Vergangenheit
- Keine Verlaufsform bei Zustandsverben und bei Antwort auf die Frage „wie viel/viele"

**A** Underline the correct form.

1 I **didn't see / hadn't seen** Frank since my first trip to Alaska in 2007.

2 When we finally got to Almaty we **had travelled / travelled** over 3000 miles.

3 I recognized Mr Li immediately although we **had never met / never met** face to face before.

4 We got to the conference centre late and the presentation **already began / had already begun**.

5 Your last company car was a Lexus, wasn't it? What **had you / had you had** before that?

6 Tessa and Mark saw what happened, **had looked / looked** at each other and burst out laughing.

**B** Make complete sentences using the simple past and the past perfect.

When / we / get to the meeting / the others / already / arrive.

*When we got to the meeting, the others had already arrived.*

1 I / already / do all the calculations / when I / leave the office yesterday evening.

2 Roland / only be on one business trip abroad before he / fly to China last year.

3 We / be all in a good mood because we / win the contract.

4 Joe / almost give up / when he finally / find a new job.

5 I / upload the photos of the factory that I / take the previous day.

6 They / not be partners very long when they / decide to go their separate ways.

**C** Complete this story using the simple past, the past progressive, the past perfect or the past perfect progressive.

Some years ago my brother Richard ............................ [1] (go) on a business trip to Baku in Azerbaijan. In those days you had to fly to Almaty near the Chinese border, then all the way back to Baku. The evening before his flight, he ............................ [2] (pack) his suitcase. While he ............................ [3] (put) in some "presents" that his boss ............................ [4] (give) him the day before for one of the Azerbaijanian officials, he suddenly ............................ [5] (think) that it might be a good idea to pack some of the stuff in his hand baggage, just in case. But in the end he ............................ [6] (not do) it because of the regulations about liquids – he ............................ [7] (have) trouble a few months earlier at an airport.

The next day, Richard ............................ [8] (get up) very early. Since the previous year when he ............................ [9] (miss) a flight to Chicago, he ............................ [10] (become) very careful about getting to the airport in good time. However, he needn't have bothered because his flight ............................ [11] (be) in fact late. He ............................ [12] (check in) his luggage straight through to Baku, ............................ [13] (go) through security, and ............................ [14] (sit) down in the departure lounge. He ............................ [15] (wait) for over 90 minutes when the departure was finally announced.

When Richard finally ............................ [16] (get) to Almaty, the connecting flight to Baku ............................ [17] (already leave). After he ............................ [18] (wait) for over 30 minutes at the airline information desk, they ............................ [19] (tell) him that he would have to stay the night and get a flight the next day. He ............................ [20] (do) this, and eventually ............................ [21] (take off) for Baku in the same clothes, unshaven, and 15 hours late. The plane ............................ [22] (land) and he ............................ [23] (go) to the baggage reclaim to collect his suitcase. He ............................ [24] (stand) by the carousel for over 20 minutes when he ............................ [25] (realize) that he was the only person without his luggage. Again he ............................ [26] (go) to the airline information desk. This time they ............................ [27] (give) him a form. After he ............................ [28] (fill it in), they ............................ [29] (tell) him that his suitcase would be delivered the next morning. He ............................ [30] (leave) the baggage hall and ............................ [31] (walk) to the meeting point where the official ............................ [32] (wait). He ............................ [33] (wait) two hours the previous day and ............................ [34] (not be) in a very good mood, although he ............................ [35] (smile) politely. Richard ............................ [36] (still wear) the same clothes he ............................ [37] (put on) the previous morning in London. He ............................ [38] (not feel) very good. And, worst of all, the suitcase with the "presents" ............................ [39] (never arrive). He later found out that the airline ............................ [40] (send) it back to London!

| | |
|---|---|
| **want to** | **I'll get** |
| Good morning. I ~~will~~ speak to Tereza Sokol, please. | Just a moment. ~~I get~~ her for you. |

## Form

- will: Kurzform 'll, Verneinung won't

You'll see Tom at the meeting tomorrow, but Ann won't be there.
Will Sonia be there? – Yes, she will. / No, she won't.

**!** **Deutsch „will/wollen" – Englisch want(s) to**

Deutsch „will/wollen" zum Ausdruck eines Wunsches entspricht want to (nicht ~~will~~.)

| | |
|---|---|
| *Ed will neue Arbeitszeiten.* | Ed **wants** (~~will~~) new working hours. |
| *Er will flexibel sein.* | He **wants to** be (~~will be~~) flexible. |

**!** **Englisch will – Deutsch Gegenwart**

Im Deutschen ist oft die Gegenwart möglich, wo im Englischen will stehen muss.

*Ich sehe dich morgen.*    I'll **see** (~~I see~~) you tomorrow.

## Vorhersagen und Vermutungen

- Mit will und won't macht man Vorhersagen über Dinge, die sicher und nicht beeinflussbar sind.
  We **will know** the management's decision tomorrow. It'**ll be** on the intranet.
  Next year our founder **will be** 80, and the company **will be** 60 years old.

  Es können auch, wie im Deutschen, Vermutungen über die Gegenwart ausgedrückt werden.
  Departure was at 8.40. They'**ll be** in the air now.  *Der Abflug war … Jetzt werden sie schon in der Luft sein.*

- Die Vorhersage/Vermutung beruht oft auf Erfahrungswerten. Mit perhaps, maybe, possibly, probably und mit I think, I expect, I suppose, I'm certain/sure kann man zeigen, wie sicher bzw. unsicher man ist. will wird oft mit diesen Ausdrücken verwendet, ebenfalls mit I hope und I'm afraid.
  There **will probably be** fewer people at this year's fair because of the recession.
  It's Sunday so I **don't expect** we'**ll have** any problems finding somewhere to park.
  I **hope** they **won't ask** me any questions that I can't answer.

## Spontane Entschlüsse

- will/won't wird gebraucht, um spontane Entschlüsse (oft Angebote) und Reaktionen auszudrücken.
  Oh, excuse me, that's my mobile phone. I'**ll just answer** (~~I just answer~~) it.
  What would you like to drink? – I **won't** (~~don't~~) **have** any alcohol, thanks. I'**ll just have** (~~I just have~~) water.
  Let me help you. I'**ll carry** (~~I carry~~) that suitcase for you.
  After the presentation there will be a reception. – Oh, I'**ll enjoy** (~~I enjoy~~) that.

## Bereitschaft

- Mit will/won't drückt man (Nicht-)Bereitschaft aus (auch z. B. als Versprechen/Drohung).
  Max **will take** (~~takes~~) us to the airport, I'm sure.
  They want to cut our coffee break, but we **won't** (~~don't~~) **let** them do it.
  Don't be late! – I'**ll be** (~~I am~~) there on time, I promise.

## Das Wichtigste in Kürze

- Deutsch „will/wollen" = want to; Englisch will entspricht „werden"
- Mit will drückt man aus: Vorhersagen; spontane Entschlüsse, z. B. Angebote; Bereitschaft

Weitere Informationen → Units 14, 15

**A** **Underline the correct form.**

**1** Can I speak to Tom, please. – Sure, **I get him** / **I'll get him.**

**2** The course is almost full. **Does anyone here still want to** / **Will anyone here still** join it?

**3** I've forgotten his name. **I'll remember it** / **I remember it** in a minute.

**4** Be more careful in future or **I don't** / **I won't** help you again.

**5** Tea or coffee? – **I have** / **I'll have** some coffee, please.

**6** **I don't want to do this,** / **I will not do this,** but I'm afraid I have to.

**B** **Make complete sentences using the will future.**

Jo's invited us to a farewell drink next week. She / be 65. *She'll be 65.*

**1** I'm busy. I / tell you later.

**2** You / probably / meet Ann at the event.

**3** If you take my notebook, I / carry the files.

**4** The situation / probably improve next month.

**5** The traffic's terrible. I hope we / not be late.

**6** I / get you some coffee if you like.

**C** **Complete these dialogues with want to or the will future.**

**1** A: I'm sorry. Mr Waites has gone out. I . . . . . . . . . . . . . . . . . . . . tell him you called.

   B: Thanks. I . . . . . . . . . . . . . . . . . . . . try again later.

**2** A: I've got such a bad headache. I think I . . . . . . . . . . . . . . . . . . . . send Miranda a mail to say that I probably

   . . . . . . . . . . . . . . . . . . . . (not) be at the Pilates class at lunchtime.

   B: I . . . . . . . . . . . . . . . . . . . . get you an aspirin – perhaps that . . . . . . . . . . . . . . . . . . . . make you feel better.

**3** A: When . . . . . . . . . . . . . . . . . . . . we find out the exact cost?

   B: I don't know, but David should be able to tell us. I . . . . . . . . . . . . . . . . . . . . probably see him this afternoon.

**4** A: The company . . . . . . . . . . . . . . . . . . . . reduce emissions and improve its carbon footprint, but they

   . . . . . . . . . . . . . . . . . . . . (not) spend a lot of money.

   B: In that case the results . . . . . . . . . . . . . . . . . . . . be minimal, and the publicity value . . . . . . . . . . . . . . . . . . . . .

   (not) be very high.

**D** **Cross out and correct the verb – if it is wrong!**

**1** They've promised that the restructuring (**doesn't happen**) . . . . . . . . . . . . . . . . . . . . before next year.

**2** I'm sure you (**are not**) . . . . . . . . . . . . . . . . . . . . surprised if I tell you that sales have been very bad.

**3** I (**give**) . . . . . . . . . . . . . . . . . . . . you a lift to the station if you like.

**4** We (**don't buy**) . . . . . . . . . . . . . . . . . . . . from that company in the future. They've let us down so often.

**5** How (**do you get**) . . . . . . . . . . . . . . . . . . . . to work tomorrow if your car is off the road?

**6** Would you like some coffee? – (**I make**) . . . . . . . . . . . . . . . . . . . . it. You just carry on with what you're doing.

**7** I hear Susan is to be the new team leader. Do you think (**you prefer**) . . . . . . . . . . . . . . . . . . . . . . . . . . . . . . . . . . . . . . .
working under her as your new boss?

**8** They've asked me to work this Sunday, but (**I don't**) . . . . . . . . . . . . . . . . . . . . do it.

**9** You've been there before. What's the best way to travel? Thomas (**will**) . . . . . . . . . . . . . . . . . . . . drive, but
I (**will**) . . . . . . . . . . . . . . . . . . . . go by train.

**10** I haven't looked at the figures yet, but I'm worried we (**don't cover**) . . . . . . . . . . . . . . . . . . . . our costs again.

**E** **Translate the following sentences. Where possible, use will.**

**1** Haben Sie die Hotline-Nummer? Ich bin sicher, dass wir sie später brauchen.

**2** Jill will mehr Geld, aber ich glaube nicht, dass sie es bekommt.

**3** Ich gebe dir einen Tipp: Such dir eine neue Stelle.

**4** Vergessen Sie nicht, Francesca zu informieren. – Nein, ich vergesse es nicht!

**5** Wenn Frau Gresham zurück ist, ruft sie Sie an.

**6** Ich helfe dir später. Ich will diesen Bericht erst fertigstellen.

**7** Ich verspreche Ihnen, es passiert nicht wieder.

> How do you plan to travel? Have you decided?

> *are going to drive*
> Yes, we ~~drive~~.

## going to

- going to wird gebraucht, um vorüberlegte Entschlüsse und Pläne auszudrücken.
  We**'re going to buy** from the Japanese, not the Chinese. We've already placed the order.
  *Wir werden von den Japanern kaufen, nicht von den Chinesen. Wir haben bereits die Bestellung abgegeben.*
  Jane **isn't going to come** back after her maternity leave. She**'s going to go** freelance and **work** from home.
  *Jane wird nach dem Mutterschutz nicht wieder kommen. Sie will sich selbständig machen und ... arbeiten.*

  Vergleiche:
  I**'m going to park** in the multi-storey. There's never a space in the short-stay. [= vorüberlegter Entschluss]
  *Ich parke im Parkhaus. In der Kurzparkzone findet man nie einen Platz.*
  Oh, look. There is a space today. OK, I**'ll park** here. [= spontaner Entschluss]
  *Ach, schau. Heute gibt es einen Platz. Gut, ich parke hier.*

- Mit going to sagt man ferner, was auf Grund bestehender Vorzeichen geschehen wird.
  Look at all this traffic. We**'re going to be** late.  *Sehen Sie sich diesen Verkehr an. Wir werden uns verspäten.*
  Careful, your bag! You**'re going to lose** your wallet! ... *Sie verlieren gleich Ihre Brieftasche!*

- Es gibt auch eine Vergangenheitsform von be going to. Mit was/were going to sagt man, was beabsichtigt war oder auf Grund bestehender Vorzeichen erwartet wurde. Oft ist aber etwas anderes eingetreten.
  Oh Miriam, hello. I **was going to phone** you later, but you've beaten me to it.
  *... Ich wollte dich später anrufen, aber du bist mir zuvorgekommen.*
  The project was behind schedule and it **was going to be** impossible to meet our deadline. But then ...
  *Das Projekt war im Verzug und es würde unmöglich sein, den Termin einzuhalten. Aber dann ...*

## Verlaufsform der Gegenwart

- Die Verlaufsform der Gegenwart verwendet man, wenn für etwas Zukünftiges bereits Vorkehrungen oder Abmachungen getroffen sind, oder wenn man für sich eine bestimmte Zeiteinteilung vorgenommen hat. Wenn sich die Verlaufsform auf die Zukunft bezieht, wird sie meist mit einer Zeitbestimmung gebraucht, z. B. tomorrow, next week, on Friday, at seven o'clock usw.
  I**'m meeting** an important client for lunch **tomorrow**. I've booked at that expensive Italian restaurant.
  I**'m taking** a day off **on Friday**, so I must get everything finished by Thursday evening.

## Einfache Form der Gegenwart

- Die einfache Form der Gegenwart verwendet man, wenn etwas durch einen Fahrplan, ein Programm usw. vorgegeben ist.
  My train **arrives** at 8.23 and the conference **starts** at 9.

> ### Das Wichtigste in Kürze
> - going to = „Das habe ich fest vor." / „Ich sehe es schon kommen."
> - was/were going to = „Das hatte ich fest vor." / „Ich sah es schon kommen."
> - Verlaufsform der Gegenwart + Zeitbestimmung = „Dafür habe ich Vorkehrungen/Abmachungen getroffen."
> - einfache Gegenwart = „Das ist durch einen Fahrplan / ein Programm vorgegeben."

Weitere Informationen ⟶ Units 13, 15

**A** Underline the correct form.

1  What **are you doing** / **do you do** this evening?
2  It's Rachel's birthday tomorrow. **I'm going to organize** / **I organize** some drinks.
3  **Are you seeing** / **Do you see** Angel Chang when you're in Taiwan next week?
4  The crisis **hits** / **is going to hit** this company sooner or later.
5  We **don't have** / **aren't having** a Christmas party this year. It's a cost-cutting measure.
6  I know what they plan to offer me, and **I'm not going to accept** / **I'm not accepting** it.

**B** Make sentences or questions with the present progressive or the simple present.
Sometimes both forms are possible.

1  I / meet / a friend after work tomorrow. .........................................................................

2  Jane's train / arrive at 11.30 or 12.30? ..........................................................................

3  We / not have a holiday this summer. We / stay here. ................................................

4  Here is a list of the people we / invite to the conference. ........................................

5  When / you give your presentation? ..............................................................................

6  What / Julie do this evening? .................................................. Does she want to join us?

**C** Complete these sentences and questions with **going to**. Sometimes you need **was/were going to**.

1  The weather ........................... (improve). It ........................... (be) a better day tomorrow.

2  Martin and Susanne ........................... (discuss) things tomorrow. The meeting is at 3.30.

   ........................... (you/be) there, too?

3  What ........................... (we/do) about this problem? We need a solution as soon as possible.

4  I ........................... (order) 1000 copies, but Janice says that's not enough.

5  We ........................... (not invite) Watkins to the meeting, but we've been told we have to.

**D** Complete these dialogues with **going to**, but use **will** where that is not possible.
Sometimes you need **was/were going to**.

1  A: I hear Maxine ................................. (do) some consultancy work when she retires.

   B: Yes, she says she ................................. (not sit) at home and do nothing.

2  A: I don't have room for this plant any more. I ................................. (throw) it away.

   B: Don't do that. I ........................... (take) it home.

3  A: Where ........................... (you/stay) this time? At that motel again?

   B: No. I ........................... (book) somewhere nearer the centre of town.

4  A: Look at the time. We ........................... (be) late.

   B: You're right. We ........................... (not be) there before ten.

5  A: I need help with my translation. I ........................... (ask) Celia, but I've heard she's away.

   B: I'm sure Amanda ........................... (help) you if you ask her nicely.

**E** Translate the following sentences.

1  Passen Sie auf! Die Leinwand *(screen)* fällt [gleich] um.
2  Ich fahre Sie, wenn Sie möchten. – Danke, aber es ist alles organisiert. Wir nehmen ein Taxi.
3  Wann fängt die Sitzung an?
4  Ich wollte Ihnen eine E-Mail schicken, aber wir können es jetzt besprechen, wenn Sie Zeit haben.
5  Ich gehe um den Block. – Gute Idee. Ich komme mit.

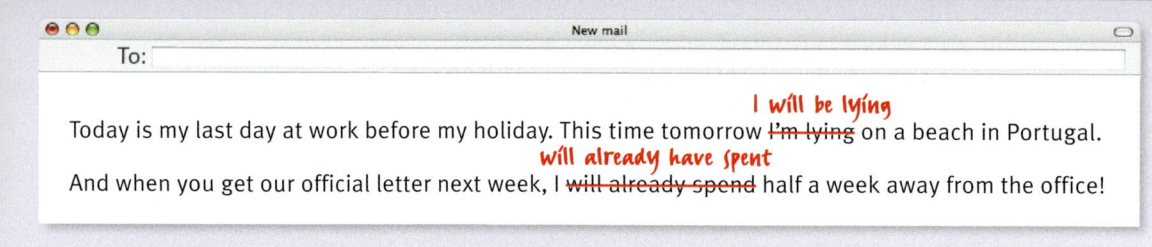

**will + Verlaufsform**

- will + Verlaufsform bildet man mit will + be ...ing.
  Next week I'**ll be travelling**. I **won't be working** from home.
  **Will** you **be meeting** Mr Li? – Yes, I **will**. / No, I **won't**.

- will + Verlaufsform hat verschiedene Verwendungen.
  - **Es kann ausdrücken, dass eine Handlung oder vorübergehende Situation zu einem zukünftigen Zeitpunkt im Verlauf begriffen, nicht abgeschlossen sein, d. h. noch andauern wird.**
    At 10.30 we **will take** our visitors round the factory. [= Um 10.30 werden wir den Rundgang beginnen.]
    At 10.45 we **will be taking** them round the factory. [= Um 10.45 werden wir gerade beim Rundgang sein.]

  - **Es kann ausdrücken, dass etwas zwangsläufig im normalen Lauf der Dinge passieren wird.**
    I'**ll be seeing** Jemma at the weekly team meeting.

  - **Es kann gebraucht werden, um besonders höflich nach Handlungen und Wünschen zu fragen.**
    At about what time **will** you **be leaving** in the morning?

  - **Es kann gebraucht werden, um Vermutungen über Ereignisse auszudrücken, die jetzt gerade im Verlauf sein müssten.**
    In the east it **will** already **be getting** light now. *Im Osten wird es jetzt schon hell werden.*

**Vollendete Zukunft**

- Die vollendete Zukunft bildet man mit will + have + Partizip Perfekt.
  By Friday I **will have completed** the report. I **won't have sent** it out.
  **Will** you **have had** feedback from anyone? – Yes, I **will**. / No, I **won't**.

  - **Mit der vollendeten Zukunft wird ausgedrückt, was bis zu einem bestimmten zukünftigen Zeitpunkt abgeschlossen sein wird. Häufiges Signalwort: by *(bis)*.**
    **By** the end of the month we'**ll** probably **have sold** over 5000.
    *Bis zum Ende des Monats werden wir wahrscheinlich mehr als 5000 verkauft haben.*

  - **Die vollendete Zukunft kann man auch verwenden, um Vermutungen über Ereignisse anzustellen, die jetzt abgeschlossen sein müssten.**
    Gerlinde's flight left at 10.40 so she **will have arrived** in London now.
    *Gerlindes Flug ging um 10.40, also wird sie jetzt in London angekommen sein.*

> **Das Wichtigste in Kürze**
> - **will be ...ing:** (1) Etwas wird zu einem zukünftigen Zeitpunkt im Gange sein
>   (2) Etwas wird zwangsläufig passieren
>   (3) Höfliche Nachfrage
>   (4) Etwas müsste jetzt gerade im Gange sein
> - **will have ...ed:** (1) Etwas wird zu einem zukünftigen Zeitpunkt abgeschlossen sein
>   (2) Etwas müsste jetzt abgeschlossen sein

Weitere Informationen ⟶ Units 13, 14

**A** Underline the correct form.

1 If you need to ask me anything, **I'll be working** / **I'll work** in Martina's office.
2 We're late. The meeting **will already start** / **will already have started** by the time we get there.
3 Don't go in yet. They started late so **they'll still be discussing** / **they'll still discuss** the budget.
4 Next Monday, 17th January, **I'll be** / **I'll have been** here for exactly five years.
5 If you call after two, **we'll finish** / **we'll have finished** lunch and I'll be free again.

**B** Make sentences using the future progressive and future perfect.

1 I always leave home at 8 o'clock and get to work at 8.45.
At 8.20 I ............................................. (travel) to work.
By 9.00 I ............................................. (arrive) at work.
2 I am in charge of a publicity event at 11 a.m. next Tuesday morning.
By Monday evening I hope I ..................................................... (organize) everything.
At exactly eleven o'clock on Tuesday I .............................................. (start) my welcoming speech.
3 Someone from the tax office is coming tomorrow.
They ............................................. (ask) awkward questions all day, I expect.
I hope they ............................................. (finish) by the time I want to go home.
4 Next Monday I am meeting a new Vietnamese business partner for the first time.
By late Sunday evening my plane ..................................................... (land) at Ho-Chi-Minh City
and I ............................................. (check in) at my hotel.
At this time on Monday morning ..................................................... (sit) in the offices of the New Saigon Trading Company.

**C** Complete these questions with the future progressive.

1 A: When ............................... (you/see) Jackson again? B: Next month probably. Why?
2 A: ............................... (you/use) the conference room? B: No, not today.
3 A: Who ........................... (you/invite) to join the team? B: Why? Are you interested?
4 A: ........................... (we / go out) to eat this evening, or do you have other plans?
B: It's up to you. What would you like to do?

**D** Complete these dialogues with the future progressive and the future perfect.
If they are not possible, use **will**.

1 A: I hope Sue ........................... (reply) to my email by the time I get back from lunch.
B: She may phone. I ........................... (let you know) if she does. Off you go, now.
2 A: I think I ....................... (check) with Diane before I give the go-ahead to the production people.
B: Don't disturb her now. She ....................... (have) her weekly meeting with the marketing team.
3 A: I ........................... (help) you set up the new system as soon as I've finished this pile of stuff.
B: Thanks, but I hope we ........................... (work things out) ourselves by then.

**E** Translate the following sentences.

1 Nächstes Jahr sind Hannah und ich schon zehn Jahre Kolleginnen.
2 Morgen um diese Zeit sitze ich im Konferenzraum in Amsterdam.
3 Die Gäste werden schon angekommen sein. Es ist schon nach 11.00.
4 Bis morgen werde ich Ihren Bericht gelesen haben.
5 Ich rufe morgen zurück. – O.k., aber bitte vormittags. Nachmittags fliege ich nach London.

> was opened          was designed by
> The new headquarters building ~~is opened~~ in 2009. It ~~is designed from~~ a British architect.

### Unterschied zwischen Aktiv und Passiv

■ In einem Aktivsatz wird gesagt, was jemand (oder etwas) aktiv tut. In einem Passivsatz wird gesagt, was mit jemandem (oder etwas) getan wird.

| | |
|---|---|
| Aktivsatz | The company **raised** its prices twice in six months. *Die Firma hat ihre Preise … erhöht.* |
| Passivsatz | Prices **were raised** twice in six months. *Die Preise wurden … erhöht.* |

Englische Passivsätze entsprechen manchmal deutschen Aktivsätzen mit „man".
I**'ve been invited** to give a lecture. *Man hat mich eingeladen, einen Vortrag zu halten.*

■ Ein Passivsatz wird oft verwendet, wenn es unwichtig, unbekannt oder offensichtlich ist, wer aktiv gehandelt hat.
The goods **have been delivered**. [Der Lieferant ist unwichtig. Wichtig ist nur, dass die Ware da ist.]
Oh look, a window **has been broken**. [Wer das Fenster kaputt gemacht hat, ist unbekannt.]
The manager **was arrested**. [Wer die Verhaftung vorgenommen hat – die Polizei – ist offensichtlich und braucht nicht extra erwähnt zu werden.]

Das Passiv wird verwendet, um Aussagen neutraler oder förmlicher wirken zu lassen.
Considerable progress **has been made**. *Erhebliche Fortschritte sind gemacht worden.*
All items **are** thoroughly **checked** before they leave the factory. *Sämtliche Artikel werden sorgfältig geprüft …*

### Form

■ Das Passiv wird mit einer Form von **be** + Partizip Perfekt gebildet.

| | |
|---|---|
| Einfache Gegenwart | Lunch **is taken** in the canteen. *Das Mittagessen wird … eingenommen.* |
| Einfache Vergangenheit | The goods **were received** yesterday. *Die Ware wurde gestern empfangen.* |
| Present Perfect | Copies **have been made**. *Kopien sind gemacht worden.* |
| Past Perfect | The budget **had been approved** earlier. *Der Finanzplan war … genehmigt worden.* |
| will-Zukunft | Your questions **will be answered**. *Ihre Fragen werden beantwortet (werden).* |

■ **be answered** im letzten Beispielsatz ist die Infinitivform des Passivs. Sie wird auch nach Modalverben wie **can, must, may, might, should** sowie nach **have to** und **going to** gebraucht.
Information **can be found** on the internet. *… findet man im Internet / sind im Internet zu finden.*
Cars **must not / may not be parked** in front of the building. *Autos dürfen nicht … abgestellt werden.*
The flight **might be cancelled** because of the snow. *Der Flug könnte … gestrichen werden.*
Nobody **has to be asked**. *Niemand muss gefragt werden.*
The old computer system **is going to be replaced** next year. *… wird nächstes Jahr ersetzt (werden).*

■ Wenn die Person, die aktiv etwas tut, in einem Passivsatz genannt wird, geschieht dies mit **by** (nicht ~~from~~).
The delegation **was welcomed by** the mayor. *Die Delegation wurde vom Bürgermeister begrüßt.*

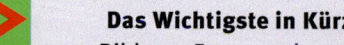

**Das Wichtigste in Kürze**
■ Bildung: Form von **be** + Partizip Perfekt (z. B. **is discussed, was made**)
Infinitiv: **be** + Partizip Perfekt (z. B. **can be found**)
■ „von/durch" = **by** (nicht ~~from~~): He was met at the airport **by** Mr Li. = *Er wurde von Herrn Li … abgeholt.*

Weitere Informationen ⟶ Units 17, 18

**A** **Underline the correct form.**

1 The company **was founded from** / **was founded by** the present owner's grandfather.
2 Talks with staff representatives **will hold** / **will be held** next week.
3 The old block **is built** / **was built** in the 1970s.
4 All windows **must closed** / **must be closed** overnight.
5 Oh no! My phone **has been stolen** / **is stolen**.

**B** **Make passive sentences.**

1 English ................................................. **(use)** throughout the company now.

2 Next year's conference ........................................................ **(hold)** in Buenos Aires.

3 Protective clothing .................................................... **(must wear)** at all times.

4 Over 300 orders .................................................. **(receive)** so far this week.

**C** **Make passive questions.**

1 the invitations / send out yet? ...........................................................

2 why / yesterday's flight / cancel? ...........................................................

3 when / the new model / launch? ...................................? Later this year?

4 the invoice / pay now? ................................. We should have paid it last week.

**D** **Say the same, using the passive. In sentences 5–8 you need by.**

1 Have they agreed a procedure yet? ⟶ Has ...........................................

2 Have we finalized the details? ⟶ Have ...........................................

3 Someone will inform you if there's a change. ⟶ You ...........................................

4 When did they reach a decision? ⟶ When...........................................

5 Tom Warner has contacted me. ⟶ I ...........................................

6 The marketing manager briefed us. ⟶ We ...........................................

7 The line manager must give permission. ⟶ Permission ...........................................

8 Your head of department has to sign the form. ⟶ The ...........................................

**E** **Complete the text with passive forms.**

How **is a book produced** (book/produce)? Most books ...........................[1] **(plan)** by the publishing

company and then authors ...............................[2] **(commission)** to write them. Very often a book

................................[3] **(have to write)** to fit into a series which ...............................[4]

**(already establish)** in the market. The process varies, but often a first version of the manuscript ........

...........................[5] **(write)**, it ...............................[6] **(then read / an editor)** and a list

of changes .......................[7] **(send)** to the author. After the manuscript ...........................[8]

**(revise)** and the revisions ...........................[9] **(accept / the publisher)**, the production process

starts – although design decisions ...............................[10] **(usually make)** earlier.

**F** **Translate the following sentences using the passive.**

1 Welche Sprache wird hier gesprochen?
2 Wann ist diese Fabrik gebaut worden?
3 Eine Entscheidung wird bald getroffen.
4 Taxis findet man am anderen Ausgang.
5 Ist der Vertrag unterschrieben worden?

> *is being extended*  *we were given*
> The factory ~~is extended~~ at the moment, so ~~us was given~~ only a short guided tour.

## Verlaufsform

■ Die Verlaufsform des Passivs bildet man mit einer Form von **be** + **being** + Partizip Perfekt.
Wie im Aktiv kennzeichnet die Verlaufsform etwas, das im Verlauf begriffen, vorübergehend ist.

Verlaufsform der Gegenwart
Aktiv: **am/are/is ...ing**      They **are preparing** the conference room now.
Passiv: **am/are/is** + **being** + Partizip Perfekt   The conference room **is being prepared** now,
       *Der Konferenzraum wird jetzt (gerade) vorbereitet.*

Verlaufsform der Vergangenheit
Aktiv: **was/were ...ing**      They **were checking** all passports.
Passiv: **was/were** + **being** + Partizip Perfekt   All passports **were being checked**.
       *Sämtliche Pässe wurden kontrolliert.*

## Das Passiv bei Verben mit zwei Objekten

■ Bestimmte Verben können zwei Objekte haben: ein direktes Objekt (meist eine Sache, die gegeben, geschickt usw. wird) und ein indirektes (meist eine Person, der etwas gegeben, geschickt usw. wird).
An ex-colleague **gave** *me* this plant when she left. We **have shown** *him* all the relevant documents.

■ In Passivsätzen mit solchen Verben kann – im Gegensatz zum Deutschen – auch die Person Subjekt des Satzes werden.
This plant **was given** *to me* by an ex-colleague. *Diese Pflanze wurde mir von einer Ex-Kollegin geschenkt.*
= *I* (~~Me~~) **was given** this plant by an ex-colleague. *Mir wurde diese Pflanze von einer Ex-Kollegin geschenkt.*
The relevant documents **have been shown** *to him*. *... sind ihm gezeigt worden. /Man hat ihm ... gezeigt.*
= *He* (~~Him~~) **has been shown** the relevant documents. *Ihm sind ... gezeigt worden. /Man hat ihm ... gezeigt.*

■ Zu den Verben, bei denen die Person Subjekt eines Passivsatzes werden kann, zählen u. a. folgende:

| | | | | | |
|---|---|---|---|---|---|
| ask | award *(vergeben)* | buy | find | give | lend |
| (e-)mail | make | offer | owe | pay | promise |
| sell | send | show | teach | tell | |

*I* **am paid** €200 each time. *Man zahlt mir jedes Mal 200€.*
*We* **will be told** the details tomorrow morning. *Uns werden die Einzelheiten morgen früh mitgeteilt.*
*Who* **was awarded** the contract? *An wen wurde der Auftrag vergeben?*

■ Bei den Verben **describe**, **explain**, **report** und **suggest** kann nur eine Sache Subjekt des Passivsatzes sein.
They **explained** the problem *to the boss*. ⋯⋙ The problem **was explained** *to the boss*.
                        ⋯⋙ ~~The boss was explained the problem.~~

## Das Wichtigste in Kürze
■ Verlaufsform: Form von **be** + **being** + Partizip Perfekt (z. B. **is being discussed**, **was being made**)
■ **I was given** = „Mir wurde gegeben": Person ist Subjekt von Passivsatz bei **give**, **send**, **show**, **tell** usw.

**A** Underline the correct form.

1 A new system **is installed** / **is being installed** at the moment.
2 **Her has been asked to leave.** / **She has been asked to leave.**
3 **I was explained the nature of the problem.** / **The nature of the problem was explained to me.**
4 When I last looked, the documents **were still copied.** / **were still being copied.**
5 **I've been given more responsibility.** / **I've given more responsibility.**

**B** Say the same, using the passive.

1 We are still analysing the results. ┅┅⟩ The results ...............................................................
2 They were asking a lot of awkward questions. ┅┅⟩ A lot .......................................................
3 Several companies are forecasting improved sales. ┅┅⟩ Improved .........................................
4 What are they discussing at the moment? ┅┅⟩ What...............................................................
5 A Chinese company is building the new headquarters. ┅┅⟩ The ...........................................

**C** Complete the text with passive forms.

Rolls Royce Limited ..............................................................[1] **(found / Charles Rolls
and Henry Royce)** in 1906, although the first Rolls Royce car ....................................[2]
**(bring)** onto the market two years previously, in 1904. The company's reputation as a producer of luxury
cars ........................................................[3] **(establish / the famous Silver Ghost model)**
which .......................................[4] **(produce)** in a new factory in the city of Derby from 1908 on.
The company also began to produce aircraft engines, and by the late 1920s car production ...............
.........................................[5] **(overtake / aircraft engine production)**. The company
grew and prospered, but in the late 1960s it ........................................................[6]
**(hit / financial problems)**. In 1971 it ..............................[7] **(nationalize)**, and two
years later the car division, which also produced Bentley cars, ......................................[8]
**(separate)** from the parent company. In 1998 Rolls Royce Motors .....................................[9]
**(sell)** to the Volkswagen Group. However, the re-privatized aero-engine company controlled the brand
name and the famous logo, and these .......................................[10] **(license)** to Volkswagen's
competitor BMW! Since 2003 Bentley cars ...............................[11] **(produce / VW)**
and Rolls Royce cars ...........................[12] **(make and sell / BMW)**.

**D** Make passive statements or questions.

1 They are giving us further training. ┅┅⟩ ...............................................................
2 How much did they pay you? ┅┅⟩ ...............................................................
3 They sent her to China for six weeks. ┅┅⟩ ...............................................................
4 Nobody told me about the meeting. ┅┅⟩ ...............................................................
5 They still haven't sent us a bill. We ┅┅⟩ ...............................................................
6 Has anyone explained the procedure to you? ┅┅⟩ ...............................................................
7 They promised us all sorts of concesssions. ┅┅⟩ ...............................................................

> 30,000 euros is a lot of money. ~~For what was it spent~~? **What was it spent on?**

### Stellung von Präpositionen in Passivsätzen

■ Das Objekt einer Präposition in einem Aktivsatz kann Subjekt in einem Passivsatz werden.
Die Präposition steht dann hinter dem Partizip Perfekt.

They **are** <u>dealing with</u> *the problem*. ⋯⟩ *The problem* **is being** <u>dealt with</u>. *Man kümmert sich um das Problem.*
We need to <u>look at</u> *costs* again. ⋯⟩ *Costs* need to **be** <u>looked at</u> again. *Kosten müssen … überprüft werden.*
How **did** they <u>arrive at</u> *the figure*? ⋯⟩ How **was** *the figure* <u>arrived at</u>? *Wie ist man auf die Zahl gekommen?*

### Infinitiv und Gerundium im Passiv

Der Infinitiv steht nach bestimmten Verben, Nomen und Adjektiven, das Gerundium nach bestimmten Verben und nach Präpositionen (siehe Units 29–31). In Passivsätzen haben Infinitiv und Gerundium eine eigene Form.

■ Der Infinitiv hat die Form **to be** + Partizip Perfekt.

The boss has asked **to be informed**. *Der Chef hat gebeten, informiert zu werden.*
This is not an opportunity **to be missed**. *Dies ist keine Gelegenheit, die man sich entgehen lassen sollte.*
When there is conflicting information, it's easy **to be misled**. *… ist es leicht, in die Irre geführt zu werden.*

■ Das Gerundium hat die Form **being** + Partizip Perfekt.

I don't like **being ignored**. *Ich habe es nicht gern, ignoriert zu werden.*
We don't mind **being paid** twice! *Wir haben nichts dagegen, zweimal bezahlt zu werden!*
I'm looking forward to **being introduced** to your team. *Ich freue mich darauf, … vorgestellt zu werden.*
We were afraid of **being stopped** by the police. *Wir hatten Angst, von der Polizei angehalten zu werden.*

### Das Passiv bei Verben des Sagens und Meinens

■ Verben des Sagens und Meinens können das unpersönliche **it** als Subjekt eines Passivsatzes haben.

**It is believed** that he is almost bankrupt. *Man glaubt, dass er fast bankrott ist.*
**It is understood** that a new offer will be made. *Man geht davon aus, dass … unterbreitet wird.*
**It was said** that prices would fall. *Es hieß / wurde gesagt, dass die Preise fallen würden.*

Zu den Verben, bei denen **it** Subjekt eines Passivsatzes sein kann, zählen u. a. folgende:

**believe   claim   expect   hope   know   report   say   show   think   understand**

■ Bei all diesen Verben außer **hope** kann auch eine Person oder Sache Subjekt des Passivsatzes werden.
Das zweite Verb steht dann im Infinitiv.

The media **say** that *the worst of the recesssion* <u>is</u> over.
⋯⟩ *The worst of the recession* **is said** <u>to be</u> over. *Berichten zufolge soll das Schlimmste … vorbei sein.*

Everyone **expected** *the board* <u>to agree</u>.
⋯⟩ *The board* **was expected** <u>to agree</u>. *Es wurde davon ausgegangen, dass der Vorstand einwilligt.*

### Das Wichtigste in Kürze

■ Verb + Präposition: Im Passiv steht die Präposition hinter dem Partizip
■ Infinitivform des Passivs: **to be** + Partizip Perfekt
■ Gerundium im Passiv: **being** + Partizip Perfekt
■ **It is thought** that Tom knows. / Tom **is thought to** know. = „Tom soll Bescheid wissen.“:
  **it** oder Person ist Subjekt des Passivsatzes bei **think, say, believe** usw.

**A** **Underline the correct form. Underline both forms if both are correct.**

1 About corruption is never spoken, / Corruption is never spoken about, but it's there.
2 A good negotiator will avoid to be / being rushed into a decision.
3 I don't know if the reports are true, but it says / it is said that the company is in financial difficulties.
4 Into the matter is being looked. / The matter is being looked into.
5 It was expected that the government would raise taxes. / The government was expected to raise taxes.
6 Can you imagine to be / being paid 100,000 dollars a week?

**B** **Say the same, using the passive.**

1 They looked after us very well. ⋯⋗ We ............................................................
2 Someone broke into the building. ⋯⋗ The building ...........................................
3 We are looking at a range of options. ⋯⋗ A range ............................................
4 We have tried out several ideas. ⋯⋗ Several ....................................................

**C** **Make questions with these items.**

1 are / being / care / of / taken / travel arrangements / your

......................................................................................................................?

2 be / how many people / shown / this plan / to / will

......................................................................................................................?

3 being / by the company / everything / is / for / paid

......................................................................................................................?

4 been / haven't / introduced / to / who / you

......................................................................................................................?

**D** **Complete the sentences with the passive form of the gerund.**

1 I can't imagine .......................... (ask) to join the team, but who knows. Maybe they will ask me.
2 My advice is this: try to avoid .......................... (draw) into an argument.
3 What are our chances of .......................... (give) more time for this project?
4 I'm afraid of .......................... (make) redundant.
5 I'm tired of .......................... (tell) the same old lies.
6 She says she objects to ...................... (treat) like a child by someone who has far less experience.

**E** **Say the same, using the passive.**

1 They say that prices are likely to rise. ⋯⋗ It ...................................................
2 We expect sales to double. ⋯⋗ Sales ...............................................................
3 They said that nobody would lose their job. ⋯⋗ It ............................................
4 We hope that the contract will be signed very soon. ⋯⋗ It ...............................
5 People believe that a Russian consortium is interested in the site. ⋯⋗ A Russian consortium ..............

......................................................................................................................

can speak some Finnish     was able to help out
I ~~can some Finnish~~, and yesterday I ~~could help out~~ at a meeting with some people from Helsinki.

### „können" zum Ausdruck einer Fähigkeit: can, be able to

- Mit can und be able to sagt man, was jemand kann oder wozu er in der Lage ist.
  can hat nur eine Gegenwarts- und Vergangenheitsform; mit be able to können alle Zeitformen gebildet werden.

| | |
|---|---|
| Gegenwart | I can read / I'm able to read menus in Spanish. *kann* |
| | I can't hold / I'm not able to hold a conversation in Spanish. *kann nicht* |
| Vergangenheit | When I was younger, I could work / I was able to work all day without a break. *konnte* |
| | I couldn't work / I wasn't able to work all night. *konnte nicht* |
| Present Perfect | I have been able to contact Tom. I haven't been able to contact Jill. *habe (nicht) können* |
| Zukunft | We will be able to meet. We won't be able to talk long. *werden (nicht) können* |

- „konnte" (Vergangenheit) wird mit could oder was/were able to ausgedrückt. Mit beiden kann man eine allgemeine Fähigkeit ausdrücken. Wenn jedoch gesagt wird, was jemandem in einer Einzelsituation gelang, kann man nur was/were able to gebrauchen.
  After six months in Rome, I could communicate / I was able to communicate in Italian quite well.
  I had a car accident one day and was able to (~~could~~) explain in Italian what had happened.

  In Fragen und verneinten Sätzen sind wiederum beide möglich.
  Could you explain / Were you able to explain what had happened?
  I couldn't explain / I wasn't able to explain what had happened.

- Mit can oder be able to wird gesagt, wozu man jetzt und zukünftig in der Lage ist.
  I can meet / I am able to meet you tomorrow for lunch.

  Nur will be able to ist möglich, wenn die Fähigkeit, etwas zu tun, jetzt noch nicht vorhanden ist.
  When I've finished the training course, I'll be able to negotiate (~~can negotiate~~) in Spanish.

- can kann – außer z. B. in Kurzantworten – nicht allein stehen (d. h. ohne ein weiteres Verb).
  I can speak French (~~can French~~). *Ich kann Französisch.*
  Will you translate this? You can do it (~~can it~~) better than me. *Sie können es besser als ich.*

### Verben der Sinneswahrnehmung

- Verben der Sinneswahrnehmung – see, hear, smell, taste, touch – stehen meist mit can oder could.
  I can see/hear/smell the sea. *Ich sehe/höre/rieche das Meer.*
  I could taste something bitter in the soup. *Ich schmeckte etwas Bitteres in der Suppe.*

> **Das Wichtigste in Kürze**
> - can hat nur zwei Formen: can (Gegenwart) und could (Vergangenheit); andere Zeitstufen: nur be able to
> - „konnte(n)" (Vergangenheit) = could oder was/were able to; einmaliges Gelingen, nur was/were able to
> - Zukunft: can oder will be able to; wenn Fähigkeit noch nicht voranden ist, nur will be able to
> - see, hear, smell, taste, touch: mit can/could bei momentaner Sinneswahrnehmung

Weitere Informationen → Units 20–24

**A** Underline the correct form. Underline both forms if both are correct.
1 What **can you see** / **see you** in this diagram?
2 **Was you able to find** / **Were you able to find** your way without satnav?
3 I **can understand** / **will be able to understand** more after the course next week.
4 Will you be able to tell me more tomorrow? – **Yes, I will.** / **Yes, I will can.**
5 **Could you find out** / **Were you able to find out** any more details?
6 Bernadette **can better English** / **can speak better English** than me.
7 In my old firm we **could take** / **were able to take** a day off if we had enough overtime.
8 When I was in Hamburg last week I **could speak** / **was able to speak** to Magda about the re-structuring.

**B** Complete the answers to these questions using **can/can't**, **could/couldn't** or a form of **be able to**.

1 A: Did you get the chance to see anything of Sydney when you were there for the conference?

B: Yes, I was there over a weekend and ............................. go to the beach.

2 A: Have you invited Carol and Jane to the meeting?

B: Well, I sent them both an email, but I ..................................... speak to either of them yet.

3 A: How was your presentation yesterday?

B: People said it was good, but I was so nervous that I ............................. judge.

4 A: How does Jemma feel about her husband's new job in the States? Is she going to get a job, too?

B: She wants to, but she ............................. look for work properly until she's got a green card.

5 A: What was your hotel like?

B: It wasn't very comfortable, but it was near the exhibition centre so I ....................... walk there.

**C** Make questions for these answers. Use **can**, **could** or a form of **be able to**.

1 A: ..................................... French?

B: No, I can't really. I only had two years of French at school.

2 A: ................................. use your presentation skills when you were in the other department?

B: Unfortunately not.

3 A: How was the flight? ..................................... sleep on the plane?

B: Yes, thanks. I slept really well.

4 A: When ................................. return to work?

B: The doctor says I need complete rest for at least ten days.

**D** Translate the following sentences.
1 Konnten Sie das Paket mit an Bord nehmen oder war es zu groß?
2 Ich sehe die Berge aus meinem Fenster.
3 Es tut mir leid. Ich habe den Bericht noch nicht übersetzen können.
4 Helfen Sie mir bitte. Ich kann es nicht alleine *(on my own)*.
5 Haben Sie schon mit Ihrem Chef sprechen können?
6 Es tut mir leid. Ich werde im Juni nicht nach Japan kommen können.
7 Hören Sie das Geräusch? – Nein, ich höre nichts.
8 Die Sitzung war ein Erfolg. Wir konnten das Management überreden, den Plan zu akzeptieren.

# Modal verbs (2): *können* to express possibility + permission
## Modalverben (2): „können" zum Ausdruck von Möglichkeit + Erlaubnis

> may/might/could
> There's a mistake somewhere. The total number of sales ~~can~~ be wrong.

### „können" zum Ausdruck einer Möglichkeit: can, may, might, could

■ Mit can drückt man eine allgemeine Möglichkeit aus. Man sagt, was immer sein kann.
It **can rain** a lot in the south of the country in winter.  *Im Süden des Landes kann es im Winter viel regnen.*

■ Wenn man sagt, was in einer konkreten Situation sein kann, verwendet man may, might oder could (nicht ~~can~~.)
Oh, the phone's ringing. It **may/might/could** (~~can~~) **be** for me. I'm expecting a call.
[= Es könnte/ kann für mich sein.]
My laptop is broken. The repair **may/might/could** (~~can~~) **be** quite expensive.
[= Die Reparatur könnte/ kann ziemlich teuer werden.]

■ Mit may not / might not (nicht ~~couldn't~~ oder ~~can't~~) drückt man aus, dass etwas möglicherweise nicht der Fall ist.
Wait and see. The repair **may not** / **might not** (~~couldn't / can't~~) **be** as expensive as you think.
[= Es könnte sein, dass die Reparatur doch nicht so teuer wird.]

■ Mit can't schließt man eine Möglichkeit aus.
Who is that next door? – It **can't be** Max. He's in Istanbul this week.  [= Es kann nicht Max sein.]

### „können" zum Ausdruck einer Erlaubnis: can, could

■ Erlaubnis kann man mit can und could ausdrücken. may („dürfen") wird auch gebraucht (siehe Unit 23).
Mit can und could bittet man um Erlaubnis. Erteilt bzw. verweigert man die Erlaubnis, muss man can bzw. can't verwenden.
**Can/Could** I **open** the window?
Mr Smith is ready. You **can go** in now.
You **can't park** here, this is private.

### Das Wichtigste in Kürze
■ Möglichkeit:
„es kann immer sein": can
„es kann in diesem Fall sein": may, might, could
„es kann sein, dass dies nicht der Fall ist": may not, might not
„es kann nicht sein": can't
■ Erlaubnis:
um Erlaubnis bitten: can/could?
Erlaubnis erteilen: can
Erlaubnis verweigern: can't

Weitere Informationen → Units 19, 21–24

**A** **Underline the correct form.**

1  The report  can / may  be true, but I don't know.
2  Ronaldo  can / might  know the latest price. I should ask him.
3  The coat is far too big. It  can't / may not  be Emma's.
4  Could I leave now? – Yes, of course you  can / could.
5  That call  can / might  be for Peter.
6  Train journeys  could / can  be quicker than you think.

**B** **Which sentences are correct: A, B, or A and B?**

1  **A** I may be a bit late tomorrow.
   **B** I might be a bit late tomorrow.

2  Where's John? – I don't know.
   **A** He can be at lunch.
   **B** He may be at lunch.

3  **A** Could I bring my trainee to the meeting?
   **B** Can I bring my trainee to the meeting?

4  Who's Tatiana talking to? – I'm not sure.
   **A** It can be Mr Li.
   **B** It could be Mr Li.

5  I'm expecting something from the design studio, so that parcel which the courier has just brought
   **A** may be for me.
   **B** might be for me.

**C** **Complete the dialogues using can, can't or may/might (not).**

1  A: Who's that with Frau Mertens?

   B: It ........................... be Ed Ferrow, the visitor from New York.

2  A: That person over there looks like Simon.

   B: It does. But it ........................... be him. He's away.

3  A: What's the matter? You ....................... be tired already! We've only been working for an hour.

   B: Well, I am, but I don't know why. It ....................... be the air in this room. I'll open a window.

4  A: How ........................... the market react to this news? What do you think?

   B: I don't know. It ........................... often be difficult to predict.

5  A: How are you planning to travel? The weather is not good and the roads ....................... be icy.

   B: If things are really bad, I ........................... go at all today, but wait till tomorrow.

**D** **Translate the following sentences.**

1  Es tut mir leid, aber Sie können Ihre Tasche nicht hier lassen.
2  Könnte ich später zurückrufen? – Natürlich können Sie das.
3  Ich würde Herrn Meyer nichts sagen. Er könnte es missverstehen.
4  Die Firma ist in Schwierigkeiten, aber sie kann nicht bankrott gehen.

> doesn't have to be        didn't have to pay
> A good hotel ~~mustn't be~~ expensive. I got a very good deal, and I ~~hadn't to pay~~ extra for breakfast.

### „müssen" zum Ausdruck einer Notwendigkeit

- Mit must und have to sagt man, was notwendig ist. must gibt es nur in der Gegenwart; mit have to können alle Zeitformen gebildet werden.

  | | |
  |---|---|
  | Gegenwart | I must / have to phone Gonzalez.  *Ich muss Gonzalez anrufen.* |
  | Vergangenheit | We had to re-book our flights.  *Wir mussten unsere Flüge umbuchen.* |
  | Present Perfect | I haven't had to do this often.  *Das habe ich nicht oft machen müssen.* |
  | Zukunft | You will have to wait.  *Sie werden warten müssen.* |

- In der Gegenwart gibt es einen Bedeutungsunterschied zwischen must und have to.
  Mit must kommt die Notwendigkeit von innen. Man drückt die eigene innere Überzeugung aus oder gibt einen Befehl, von dessen Richtigkeit man überzeugt ist.
  I really must give up smoking.    Boss: You must be here by 8.30.

  Mit have to kommt die Notwendigkeit von außen. Man berichtet, was von anderen angeordnet wurde oder was durch äußere Umstände, Regeln und Vorschriften bestimmt ist.
  The doctor says I have to give up smoking.   I have to be in the office by 8.30.    I have to get a visa.

**!** Die Verneinung („nicht müssen") wird mit don't/doesn't have to (nicht ~~must not~~) gebildet, oder man verwendet don't/doesn't need to (= „nicht brauchen") bzw. needn't.
I don't have to / don't need to / needn't go yet.  *Ich muss noch nicht / brauche noch nicht zu gehen.*
You don't have to / don't need to / needn't worry.  *Sie müssen/brauchen sich nicht zu sorgen.*

must not entspricht „nicht dürfen"! Damit drückt man ein Verbot oder eine dringende Empfehlung aus, auch gegenüber sich selbst.
You mustn't touch this surface.  *Sie dürfen diese Fläche nicht mit der Hand berühren.*
I mustn't forget to reply to that email.  *Ich darf nicht vergessen, diese E-Mail zu beantworten.*

- Fragen mit must sind selten. Fehler kann man vermeiden, wenn man immer have to verwendet. Dabei kommt eine Form von do zum Einsatz. Kurzantworten stehen nur mit einer Form von do.
  Do you have to go? – Yes, I do. / No, I don't.

- Mit had to („musste[n]") sagt man, was in der Vergangenheit nötig war. Die Verneinung („musste[n] nicht") heißt didn't have to oder didn't need to. In Fragen und Kurzantworten kommt did zum Einsatz.
  I had to wait. Did you and Malcolm have to wait too? – Yes, we did. / No, we didn't.
  Parking was free. We didn't have to / didn't need to pay.  *Wir mussten nicht / brauchten nicht zu zahlen.*

### Andere Entsprechungen von „müssen"

- Wie „müssen" wird must gebraucht, um Schlussfolgerungen und Annahmen auszudrücken.
  You must be Max. I've heard a lot about you.  *Sie müssen Max sein. Ich habe viel von Ihnen gehört.*

### Das Wichtigste in Kürze

- must gibt es nur in der Gegenwart; Ersatzverb: have to (Fragen, Kurzantworten und Verneinung mit do)
- must = „ich bestimme das" oder „ich halte das für nötig"; have to = „das wird von außen so bestimmt"
- „nicht müssen" = don't/doesn't have/need to oder needn't
- mustn't = „nicht dürfen"

Weitere Informationen → Units 19, 20, 22–24

**A** **Underline the correct form. Underline both forms if both are correct.**
1  I  mustn't  /  needn't  forget to switch off the photocopier.
2  You  mustn't  /  don't have to  help if you don't have time.
3  I  didn't have to  /  hadn't to  work last weekend.
4  We  don't have to  /  needn't  leave yet. There's still plenty of time.
5  There  must be  /  has to be  a mistake. I'm Martin Owen, not Michael Owen!
6  Does Martin have to be told? –  Yes, he does.  /  Yes, he has.
7  Had you to wait  /  Did you have to wait  long for an answer?

**B** **Complete these sentences with musn't or don't/doesn't have to.**
1  She ..................................... ask for permission for purchases under €2000.
2  You ..................................... tell anyone what I told you. It's just between you and me.
3  I ..................................... go to the meeting tomorrow. They don't need me.
4  I ..................................... forget to make a back-up copy.
5  You ..................................... leave things like that lying around. There's a lot of theft in the building.
6  Someone like Alan ..................................... worry about money. His partner has lots of it.
7  We leave at 9.15. You ..................................... be late.

**C** **Make questions for these answers. Use a form of have to.**
1  A: ..................................... wait long?
   B: No, the train was on time.
2  A: What time does the presentation start? When ..................................... be there?
   B: Well, we shouldn't leave it too late otherwise we won't get a seat.
3  A: ..................................... work between Christmas and New Year?
   B: No, it was the first year when I didn't.
4  A: When ..................................... go?
   B: Quite soon. My flight leaves at 2.40.
5  A: Do you think we ..................................... show our passes when we go in?
   B: Well, last time I did. So I expect we will have to this time too.
6  A: ..................................... deal with this sort of problem before?
   B: No, I haven't. It's the first time.

**D** **Translate the following sentences.**
1  Morgen muss ich nicht arbeiten.
2  Mussten Sie das sagen?!
3  Es ist schade, dass Sie jetzt schon fahren müssen. Nächstes Mal müssen Sie länger bleiben.
4  Es ist nett von Ihnen, aber Sie müssen nicht auf mich warten.
5  In unserer Abteilung haben wir viel zu tun. Müssen wir an der Marketing-Sitzung teilnehmen?

# Modal verbs (4): *können* and *müssen* in the past
## Modalverben (4): „können" und „müssen" in der Vergangenheit

> *may/might/could have left*
> I don't know where the document can be. I ~~can have left~~ it upstairs.

### „können" zum Ausdruck einer Möglichkeit in der Vergangenheit

- Um darüber zu spekulieren, was möglicherweise geschehen sein könnte, verwendet man may/might/ could have + Partizip Perfekt (aber nicht ~~can have~~).
  Ed left here very late. He **may/might/could have missed** his flight.
  *Er könnte seinen Flug verpasst haben.*

- Um zu sagen, dass etwas theoretisch hätte geschehen können (aber nicht geschehen ist), verwendet man nur might/could have + Partizip Perfekt (aber nicht ~~can have~~ oder ~~may have~~).
  The firm is bankrupt. It **might/could have survived** with better marketing. *Die Firma ist bankrott. Sie hätte mit besserem Marketing (vielleicht) überleben können. [In Wirklichkeit hat sie aber nicht überlebt.]*

- Um zu sagen, dass etwas theoretisch nicht hätte geschehen können, verwendet man couldn't have + Partizip Perfekt.
  Forty years ago you **couldn't have booked** online because the internet didn't exist.
  *Vor vierzig Jahren hätte man nicht online reservieren können, weil das Internet nicht existierte.*

### „müssen" zum Ausdruck einer Notwendigkeit in der Vergangenheit

- Um zu sagen, dass man etwas in der Vergangenheit hätte tun müssen (aber nicht getan hat), verwendet man should have / ought to have + Partizip Perfekt (siehe Unit 24).
  I'm leaving. Sorry, I **should have / ought to have told** you earlier. *… ich hätte es dir früher sagen müssen.*

- Um zu sagen, dass man etwas in der Vergangenheit nicht hätte tun müssen/brauchen (aber man hat es getan), verwendet man needn't have + Partizip Perfekt.
  I **needn't have worried** about missing my flight. It was delayed anyway. *Ich hätte mir keine Sorgen machen müssen, dass ich meinen Flug verpasse. Er war sowieso verspätet.*

### Schlussfolgerungen über die Vergangenheit

- Mit can't have + Partizip Perfekt sagt man, was nicht gewesen sein kann.
  Nobody wanted to make concessions. The negotiations **can't have been** easy. *Keiner wollte Zugeständnisse machen. Die Verhandlungen können nicht leicht gewesen sein.*

- Mit must have + Partizip Perfekt sagt man, was geschehen sein muss.
  You've finally arrived. You **must have had** a terrible journey. *Sie müssen eine schreckliche Fahrt gehabt haben.*

> ### Das Wichtigste in Kürze
> - Möglichkeit in der Vergangenheit
>   „es kann/könnte so gewesen sein": may/might/could have + Partizip Perfekt
>   „es hätte theoretisch so sein können, war aber anders": might/could have + Partizip Perfekt
>   „es hätte so nicht sein können und war auch nicht so": couldn't have + Partizip Perfekt
> - Notwendigkeit in der Vergangenheit
>   „ich hätte müssen": I should / ought to have + Partizip Perfekt
>   „ich hätte nicht müssen": I needn't have + Partizip Perfekt
> - Schlussfolgerungen
>   „es kann nicht so gewesen sein": can't/couldn't have + Partizip Perfekt
>   „es muss so gewesen sein": must have + Partizip Perfekt

Weitere Informationen → Units 19–21, 23, 24

**A** Underline the correct form.

1 Tina has a meeting in town at 4.30. She  can have already left  /  may have already left.

2 The meeting had nothing to do with our department. I  needn't have gone  /  mustn't have gone  to it.

3 We're hopelessly behind schedule. We  must have finished  /  should have finished  this last month.

4 They  can have sent  /  could have sent  the samples in the normal mail. Maybe that's why we haven't got them yet.

5 There's a lot of fog. It's possible that Rebecca  may not have reached  /  can't have reached  Brussels yet.

**B** Say what **might** or **might not** have happened. Use these verbs: **be delayed, not have, not read, not see.**

1 A: Mr Roberts hasn't made any comment about my report.

B: He ..................................... it yet.

2 A: The visitors still haven't arrived.    B: Their flight .......................................

3 A: Mrs Jakobs still hasn't revised the budget.    B: She ...................................... time.

4 A: Some companies did better in the recession than others.

B: They ....................................... it coming and taken measures to combat it early.

**C** Complete the sentences with **couldn't have** + past participle.

1 I ...................................... (do) this without your help. Thank you very much indeed.

2 The overall economic situation was difficult and so we ................................. (raise) our prices.

3 What happened was unbelievable! It ...................................... (happen) in any other country.

4 I'm so sorry to hear that you're leaving. I ...................................... (have) a better colleague.

**D** Complete the sentences with **needn't have** + past participle. Use these verbs: **leave, take, worry, write.**

1 I .................................. so much cash. I was able to pay by credit card almost everywhere.

2 Maria ................................. . Her boss was in a really good mood.

3 We have time to spare before the meeting starts. We ................................. our hotel so early.

4 I .................................. so much. Nobody will read the report anyway.

**E** Complete with **can't have** or **must have** + past participle.

1 The hotel can't be this far out of town. We ........................... (pass) it. We'll have to turn round.

2 You only started ten minutes ago! You ................................. (finish) the meeting already!

3 There's been so much snow. You ................................. (have) an easy journey.

4 It ......................... (cost) a lot to rent offices in the city centre. I'm not surprised they moved out.

5 The goods ................................. (arrive) in Hamburg yet. They only left Hong Kong yesterday.

6 You ................................. (see) a lot of changes here if you've worked here for over 30 years.

7 They ......................... (know) about this before. Otherwise how were they able to react so fast?

**F** Translate the following sentences.

1 Gut gemacht! Es kann nicht leicht gewesen sein.

2 Ich hätte Ihnen nicht helfen können. Ich war an dem Tag nicht hier.

3 Die Ergebnisse müssen super gewesen sein. Alle sind zufrieden.

4 Ich hätte mich nicht so beeilen müssen.

# 23 Modal verbs (5): *dürfen* to express permission + assumption
## Modalverben (5): „dürfen" zum Ausdruck von Erlaubnis + Annahmen

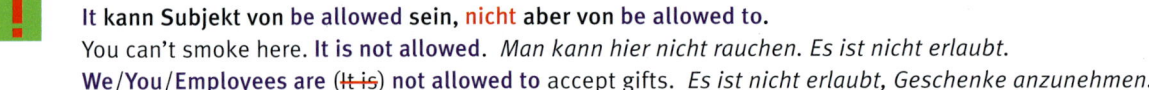

Employees are not allowed to
~~It is not allowed to~~ eat or drink
in the laboratory.

### „dürfen" zum Ausdruck einer Erlaubnis: may, might, be allowed to

- Erlaubnis drückt man mit may, might und be allowed to aus, häufig aber auch mit can = „können" (siehe Unit 20).
  Mit may und might kann um Erlaubnis gebeten werden. might („dürfte[n]") ist zurückhaltender.
  **May/Might** I **ask** a question?  *Darf/Dürfte ich eine Frage stellen.*

- Mit may wird Erlaubnis erteilt, mit may not ein Verbot ausgesprochen. Beide sind förmlich.
  Members of staff **may (not) smoke** in the courtyard.  *Mitarbeiter/innen dürfen (nicht) auf dem Hof rauchen.*

  Verbote spricht man jedoch meist mit must not aus (siehe Unit 21).

- Mit be allowed to wird berichtet, was von anderen erlaubt wird bzw. durch Vorschrift bestimmt ist.
  We'**re not allowed to smoke** in the courtyard.  *Wir dürfen nicht auf dem Hof rauchen.*
  Passengers **are not allowed to use** mobiles on board.  *Fluggäste dürfen keine Handys an Bord benutzen.*

- may hat nur eine Gegenwartsform; mit be allowed to werden die anderen Zeitformen gebildet.
  Vergangenheit    We **were allowed to** phone the embassy.  *Wir durften die Botschaft anrufen.*
  Present Perfect    I **have been allowed to** disclose this information.  *Ich habe ... enthüllen dürfen.*
  Zukunft    We **won't be allowed to** video the meeting.  *Wir werden ... nicht aufzeichnen dürfen.*

**!** It kann Subjekt von be allowed sein, nicht aber von be allowed to.
You can't smoke here. **It is not allowed.**  *Man kann hier nicht rauchen. Es ist nicht erlaubt.*
**We/You/Employees are** (~~It is~~) **not allowed to** accept gifts.  *Es ist nicht erlaubt, Geschenke anzunehmen.*

### Andere Bedeutungen von „dürfen"

Schätzungen und Annahmen mit „dürfte(n)" werden mit should und ought to wiedergegeben (siehe Unit 24).
This piece of equipment **shouldn't / oughtn't cost** more than about €2000.
*Dieses Gerät dürfte nicht mehr als etwa 2000€ kosten.*

### Das Wichtigste in Kürze
- „dürfen" zum Ausdruck von Erlaubnis
  um Erlaubnis bitten: may/might
  Erlaubnis erteilen: may
  Erlaubnis förmlich verweigern: may (not)
  Sonst: be allowed to
- „es ist (nicht) erlaubt" + Infinitiv = Person + be allowed to (~~it is [not] allowed to~~)
- „dürfte(n)" zum Ausdruck von Schätzungen und Annahmen: should / ought to

**A** Underline the correct form.

1 It's / **You're** not allowed to park here.
2 Staff **may not** / **might not** leave personal items in the reception area.
3 We **aren't allowed to** / **may not** stick pictures on the walls.
4 Company rules say that taxis **may** / **might** be used for travel to the airport.
5 **Will it** / **Will we** be allowed to ask questions at the end?

**B** Which sentences are correct: A, B, or A and B?

1 **A** We may not turn overtime into holiday.  **B** We aren't allowed to turn overtime into holiday.

2 **A** Only heads of department may enter the building at the weekend.  **B** Only heads of department must enter the building at the weekend.

3 **A** Drinks may not be placed on this surface.  **B** Drinks must not be placed on this surface.

4 **A** May I see those figures again, please?  **B** Can I see those figures again, please?

5 **A** We shouldn't need more than an hour for the meeting.  **B** We oughtn't to need more than an hour for the meeting.

6 **A** May we invite you to dinner one evening?  **B** Might we invite you to dinner one evening?

**C** Make sentences with a form of **be allowed to.**

1 Of course ................................. **(I not tell)** you my password. I'd get into big problems if I did.
2 ................................. **(we not send)** private emails, but .................................
   **(we receive)** them.
3 Jason has been arrested by the police. ................................. **(he not speak)** to a lawyer yet.
4 ................................. **(you/take)** photos? – No, they didn't let us.
5 The flight next week is an intercontinental one, so how much luggage .................................
   **(we/take)**?

**D** Correct these sentences. Use the words in brackets.

1 ~~It wasn't allowed to see the research laboratory.~~ (we)
   .................................................................
2 ~~Was it allowed to talk to any of the technical staff?~~ (you)
   .................................................................
3 ~~It isn't allowed to be a member of a trade union.~~ (employees in the company)
   .................................................................
4 ~~Will it be allowed to extend the existing building?~~ (the company)
   .................................................................

I arrived to give my presentation, but nothing was ready. There ~~should be~~ **should have been** a projector, but there wasn't.

### „sollen" zum Ausdruck von Rat und Verpflichtung: should, ought to, be supposed to

■ Mit should und ought to gibt man einen Rat oder sagt, wozu jemand verpflichtet ist (auch man selbst, nach eigener innerer Überzeugung). should und ought to sind gleichbedeutend.
You **should be** / **ought to be** more careful. *Sie sollten vorsichtiger sein.*
We **shouldn't use** / **oughtn't to use** the car so much. *Wir sollten das Auto nicht so viel benutzen.*

■ Mit be supposed to spricht man über eine Vorgabe oder Anweisung von außen oder sagt, wie etwas normalerweise gehandhabt wird.
We**'re supposed to wear** a suit and tie when we visit customers. *Wir sollen Anzug und Krawatte tragen, …*
I**'m not supposed to tell** anyone, so keep it to yourself. *Ich soll es keinem sagen, also behalt es für dich.*

Bei Vorgaben und Handhabungen in der Vergangenheit verwendet man was/were supposed to.
Anyone who wants to take part in the course **was supposed to sign up** by the end of last week.
*Wer an dem Kurs teilnehmen will, sollte sich bis Ende letzter Woche einschreiben.*

be supposed to wird nicht in der Zukunftsform oder dem Present Perfect gebraucht.

■ Mit should have / ought to have + Partizip Perfekt drückt man aus, was hätte geschehen sollen (aber nicht geschehen ist).
I'm sorry. I **should have given** / **ought to have given** you this last week. But I forgot.
*Es tut mir leid. Ich hätte Ihnen dies letzte Woche geben sollen. Aber ich habe es vergessen.*

### Andere Entsprechungen von „sollen" im Überblick

| | | |
|---|---|---|
| Sagen, was man annimmt oder erwartet | should / ought to | It **should cost** / **ought to cost** about €100.<br>*Es sollte/müsste/dürfte etwa 100€ kosten.* |
| Sagen, was angeblich sein soll | be said to / supposed to | The new boss **is said/supposed to be** very nice.<br>*Die neue Chefin soll angeblich sehr nett sein.* |
| Sagen, was fest vorgesehen ist | be to | As part of the recovery plan one factory **is to close**.<br>*Als Teil des Sanierungsplans soll eine Fabrik schließen.* |
| Fragen, was gewünscht ist | shall/should? | **Shall/Should I ask** Miriam? *Soll(te) ich Miriam fragen?* |

Man kann auch mit want + Objekt + Infinitiv nach Wünschen fragen (siehe Unit 32).
Do you **want me to do** that for you? *Soll ich das für Sie erledigen?*

Man kann auch mit tell + Objekt + Infinitiv berichten, was gewünscht ist/war (siehe Unit 32).
The secretary **told me to wait**. *Die Sekretärin sagte mir, ich solle warten.*

**Das Wichtigste in Kürze**
■ Rat und Verpflichtung: should / ought to
■ Über Vorgaben oder Anweisungen von außen berichten: be supposed to
■ „hätte sollen": should have / ought to have + Partizip Perfekt
■ Sonstige Bedeutungen:
„sollte vermutlich": should / ought to
„soll angeblich": be said to / supposed to
„soll nach Plan": be to
„soll ich?": shall/should I?

Weitere Informationen → Units 19–23

**A** Underline the correct form. Underline both forms if both are correct.

1 My boss **should** / **was supposed to** sign the form, but he didn't.

2 If we leave at 6.30, that **should** / **ought to** give us enough time to get to the airport.

3 If you ask me, they **should have fired** / **ought to have fired** Watkins ages ago.

4 Who **should clear up** / **was supposed to clear up** after yesterday's presentation?

**B** Make sentences. You need to add **should, shouldn't, ought to** or **ought not to**.

1 you / leave any valuables in your office

..................................................................................................

2 we / check with the boss before we do anything

..................................................................................................

3 Thomas / be more careful with his comments

..................................................................................................

4 we / do business with unreliable companies like that

..................................................................................................

5 on a Sunday it / be difficult to find somewhere to park

..................................................................................................

**C** Complete the sentences with a form of **be supposed to**.

1 Male and female employees ............................... be paid the same, but often they're not.

2 Nobody told me when the meeting ............................... start, so how ............

I ............................... know?

3 The courier ............................... deliver the package yesterday.

4 We ............................... produce a new plan by Friday. It's impossible!

5 I'm new here. Can you tell me who I ......................... inform when something like this happens?

**D** Complete the sentences with **should have** + past participle. Use these verbs: **arrive, not happen, tell, not be treated**.

1 The goods ................................................. by now, but they haven't.

2 Management ................................................. us about the plans earlier. Why didn't they?

3 How could they fire Mr Smith like that? He ................................................. like that

after 30 years in the firm.

4 I'm sorry, this ................................................. . I don't know whose fault it is.

**E** Complete the translation.

1 *Es sollte keinen Unterschied machen, wer welchen Kunden bedient.*

It ............................... make any difference who serves which customer.

2 *Im Ausland zu produzieren, soll billiger sein, aber das ist nicht immer der Fall.*

It ............................... be cheaper to produce abroad, but it's not always the case.

3 *Die Sitzung sollte um neun beginnen, aber um zehn nach war immer noch keiner da.*

The meeting ............................... begin at nine, but at ten past there was still nobody there.

4 *Sie wollen später dazukommen? Das sollte kein Problem sein.*

You want to join us later? That ............................... be a problem.

> set up a two-day export sales conference     call it off
> We ~~set~~ a two-day export sales conference ~~up~~ but then had to ~~call off it~~.

## Phrasal Verb = Verb + Adverb

■ Mit Phrasal Verb ist eine Einheit gemeint, die sich aus Verb + Adverb zusammensetzt.
Can you **bring** the delivery date **forward**? *Können Sie den Liefertermin vorziehen?*
The deal **fell through**. *Das Geschäft platzte.*

■ Die Bedeutung ist manchmal aus den zwei Elementen ableitbar; manchmal handelt es sich um einen idiomatischen Ausdruck.
The company **brought in** a consultant. *Die Firma hat einen Unternehmensberater hinzugezogen.*
We **get along** well. *Wir kommen gut miteinander aus.*

| | |
|---|---|
| The machine could **break down**. *kaputt gehen* | **put forward** a proposal *unterbreiten* |
| **break off** negotiations *abbrechen* | **put off** a meeting *verschieben* |
| **bring** a meeting **forward** *vorziehen* | **run down** production *zurückfahren* |
| **bring in** an expert *hinzuziehen* | Oil will **run out**. *zu Ende gehen* |
| **bring up** a subject *ansprechen* | A strike **set** production **back**. *verzögern* |
| **call** somebody **back** *zurückrufen* | **set off** on a journey *aufbrechen* |
| **call off** a meeting *absagen* | **set up** a meeting *organisieren* |
| **carry on** without me *weitermachen* | **take down** an address *aufschreiben, notieren* |
| **carry out** a survey *durchführen* | **take in** what someone is saying *erkennen,* |
| How did this **come about**? *zustande kommen* | *verstehen* |
| **draw up** a schedule *aufstellen* | **take on** more work *übernehmen* |
| The deal **fell through**. *platzen* | **take over** a firm *übernehmen* |
| We **get along** well. *miteinander auskommen* | **take up** what was said earlier *(wieder) aufgreifen* |
| I couldn't **get through**. *[am Telefon] durchkommen* | **turn** an offer **down** *ablehnen* |
| **make up** a name *erfinden* | Max **turned up**. *aufkreuzen, erscheinen* |
| **make up** an order *zusammenstellen* | |

■ Zu den Verben, die solche Verbindungen eingehen, gehören viele sehr häufig gebrauchte wie **bring, call, come, get, make, put, run, set, take, turn**.

■ Ein Objekt kann grundsätzlich zwischen dem Verb und dem Adverb oder hinter dem Adverb stehen.
We'll have to **call** <u>the meeting</u> **off**. / We'll have to **call off** <u>the meeting</u>.

Ist das Objekt lang (z. B. ein Nebensatz), steht es hinter dem Adverb.
We **carried out** <u>some extremely costly research</u>.     I **took on** <u>more than I could manage</u>.

Ist das Objekt ein Pronomen, so kann es nur zwischen Verb und Adverb stehen.
Objekt = Nomen     Who **brought** <u>this subject</u> **up**? / Who **brought up** <u>this subject</u>?
Objekt = Pronomen     Who **brought** <u>it</u> **up**? / ~~Who brought up it?~~

■ Es gibt auch Verbindungen aus Verb + Adverb + Präposition.

| | |
|---|---|
| It all **comes down to** money. *hinauslaufen auf* | **get on with** my work *voranmachen mit* |
| **come in for** a lot of criticism *viel Kritik ernten* | **go back on** a promise *nicht einhalten* |
| **come up with** a new design *erfinden* | **look forward to** seeing someone *sich freuen auf* |
| **cut back on** spending *kürzen* | **make up for** lost time *aufholen* |
| **do away with** import controls *verzichten auf* | **put up with** a bad situation *ertragen* |
| **face up to** a situation *sich stellen* | **run up against** unexpected problems *stoßen auf* |

**Das Objekt steht bei solchen Verbindungen immer hinter der Präposition.**

**A** Underline the correct form or sentence.

1 Have you **set off** / **set up** a schedule for the project yet?
2 It looks as though we will have to **call away** / **call off** the visit.
3 It's a good plan, but do we have enough people to **carry it out** / **carry out it**?
4 They say they are going to **do away** / **do away with** a lot of the bureaucracy.
5 We have to **bring about** / **bring forward** the product launch by two weeks.
6 They have **put forward an extremely ambitious plan that will cost millions.** /
  **put an extremely ambitious plan that will cost millions forward.**

**B** Fill in the correct adverb. Use each one only once.

| along • back • off • out • over • through • up |
| :---: |

1 I've been trying to contact our representative in Uganda, but I just can't get ...................

2 It's really important in a team that everyone gets ................... with each other.

3 If you don't want to accept an invitation, but don't want to say 'no', you have to make ...................

  an excuse.

4 Mr Li said there was no way he could agree to our terms and broke the negotiations ...................

5 If I have to leave early, could you take ...................?

6 We have to hurry. Time is running ...................

7 Are you leaving now? When will you get ...................?

**C** Does the object in brackets go in position A or position B? Or are A and B both possible?

1 (the building work)        Bad weather has set **A** [   ] back **B** [   ] by two weeks.
2 (two more people with a
  lot of experience of the
  Malaysian market)          My line manager has decided to bring **A** [   ] in **B** [   ].
3 (it)                       I had an invitation to stay on for the weekend, but I turned **A** [   ] down **B** [   ].
4 (the decision)             We need more time so I think it's wiser to put **A** [   ] off **B** [   ].
5 (your details)             Just a moment, I'll get someone to take **A** [   ] down **B** [   ].
6 (them)                     I thought Sarah's ideas were very good, but nobody took **A** [   ] up **B** [   ].

**D** Replace the verb in brackets by a phrasal verb or a phrasal verb + preposition that means the same.

| Verbs: call • come • come, cut • fall • take |
| :---: |
| Adverbs & prepositions: about • back • in • off • on • through • up • with |

1 I've decided to (cancel) .......... .......... my trip to Pakistan.

2 We're going to have to (reduce) .......... .......... .......... costs.

3 I don't know how these marketing people can (invent) .......... .......... .......... new product

  names all the time.

4 The system had never broken down before and the engineers were trying to find out how a total system

  failure like that could (happen) .......... ...........

5 I was tired and jet-lagged and couldn't (understand) .......... .......... what the taxi driver was saying.

6 Unless the two partners in a joint venture respect each other, the project will (collapse) .......... ..........

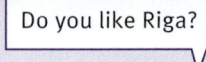

Do you like Riga?

*do*
Yes, I ~~like~~. It's a great city.

*do you do*
So what ~~do you~~ in your spare time?

### Fragebildung mit und ohne do

■ Wenn ein Aussagesatz ein Hilfsverb enthält, bildet man die dazugehörige Frage (wie im Deutschen) durch Umstellung von Subjekt und Verb. Steht ein Vollverb (außer be) im Aussagesatz, muss eine Form von do (do, does oder did) als Hilfsverb eingesetzt werden.

| | | |
|---|---|---|
| – Hilfsverben zur Zeitenbildung: be, have, will<br>Frage: Hilfsverb + Subjekt + Vollverb | Tom **is** coming. ⟶<br>Tom **was** running. ⟶<br>Tom **has** left. ⟶<br>Tom **will** be late. ⟶ | **Is** Ann coming?<br>**Was** Ann running?<br>**Has** Ann left?<br>**Will** Ann be late? |
| – Modale Hilfsverben: can, should, may, might usw.<br>Frage: Hilfsverb + Subjekt + Vollverb | Tom **can** come. ⟶<br>Tom **should** wait. ⟶ | **Can** Ann come?<br>**Should** Ann wait? |
| – be als Vollverb – Frage: Form von be + Subjekt | Tom **is** English. ⟶ | **Is** Ann English? |
| – Vollverben außer be<br>Frage: Hilfsverb do/does/did + Subjekt + Vollverb | Tom **knows** Mr Li. ⟶<br>Tom **phoned**. ⟶ | **Does** Ann **know** Mr Li?<br>**Did** Ann **phone**? |

■ Fragen mit dem Vollverb have werden mit do/does/did gebildet, Fragen mit have got jedoch ohne.
Tom **has** time. ⟶ **Does** Ann **have** time?
Tom **has got** time. ⟶ **Has** Ann **got** time?

### Kurzantworten

■ Ein schlichtes Yes oder No als Antwort kann abrupt und unhöflich wirken, deshalb wird oft eine sogenannte Kurzantwort verwendet. Dabei wird das Hilfsverb der Frage wieder aufgegriffen.
**Is** Piotr coming? – Yes, he **is**. / No, he **isn't**.
**Was** Mia waiting? – Yes, she **was**. / No, she **wasn't**.
**Has** my letter arrived? – Yes, it **has**. / No, it **hasn't**.
**Will** it be cold? – Yes, it **will**. / No, it **won't**.
**Can** you see? – Yes, I **can**. / No, I **can't**.
**Do** you ski? – Yes, I **do**. / No, I **don't**.
**Does** Janet know? – Yes, she **does**. / No, she **doesn't**.
**Did** it rain? – Yes, it **did**. / No, it **didn't**.

■ Auch bei Fragen mit dem Vollverb be und have got wird das Verb der Frage wiederholt.
**Is** Tony here? – Yes, he **is**. / No, he **isn't**.
**Have** you got time? – Yes, I **have**. / No, I **haven't**.

### Das Wichtigste in Kürze

■ Fragen mit einem Vollverb: Form von do verwenden
■ Komplette Kurzantworten sind höflicher – Hilfsverb der Frage wiederholen

Weitere Informationen ⟶ Units 27, 28

**A** **Underline the correct form.**

1 Where  is the presentation taking place  /  the presentation is taking place?
2 Have you seen  /  You have seen  Max today? I can't find him anywhere.
3 Can you help me? –  Yes, I can.  /  Yes, I help.
4 Do you have got  /  Have you got  your own office?
5 Were people waiting? –  Yes, they did.  /  Yes, they were.
6 What does your colleague do?  /  What does your colleague?  – She looks after the Maxpro account.

**B** **Make questions to fit the answers. You need a form of do in all of them. Use the phrases in the box.**

> do • get to work • involve all the team • like living in Beijing • start work here

1 A: How ...................................................? B: I commute by train.

2 A: When ..............................................? B: Four years ago. Before that I worked in Munich.

3 A: .....................................................? B: No, I hated it.

4 A: ............................................... in the decision-making process?

   B: Yes, she's a good boss. She rarely decides anything without consulting us.

5 A: What ...............................................? B: I'm an IT specialist.

**C** **Give short answers for the following questions.**

1 A: Do you like your new job? B: Yes, .............................

2 A: Are Hans and Hannah coming to the meeting? B: Yes, .............................

3 A: Did Paul phone back yesterday? B: No, .............................

4 A: Have the lawyers been in touch? B: Yes, .............................

5 A: Does Sue need help? B: No, .............................

6 A: Can you work this machine? B: No, .............................

**D** **Make questions and short answers. Be careful with the different tenses!**

1 you / know where Andrea is? – No, I'm sorry, I / not.

   ..............................................................................................

2 Dr Schneider and her guests / come back from lunch yet? – Yes.

   ..............................................................................................

3 you / finish that report yesterday? – Yes.

   ..............................................................................................

4 Petra / come tomorrow? – No, I'm afraid she / not.

   ..............................................................................................

5 you / have time to help me now? – Yes.

   ..............................................................................................

6 Max / meet Mr Li last week? – No, he / not

   ..............................................................................................

**E** **Translate the following questions and short answers.**

1 Hast du mein Handy gesehen? – Nein.
2 Warst du gestern auf der Messe? – Ja.
3 Gehen Sie heute Abend zum Vortrag? – Ja.
4 Haben Sie die E-Mail-Adresse? – Ja.

> Who do you work with?
> ~~With who you work?~~

> Nobody! It's just me.

### wh-Fragen mit und ohne do

■ Fragen mit when, where, how und why werden mit einer Form von do gebildet, wenn sonst kein Hilfsverb vorhanden ist.

|  | Tom | works | at home | on Wednesdays. |
|---|---|---|---|---|
| When does | Tom | work | at home? |  |
| Where does | Tom | work |  | on Wednesdays? |

■ who-Fragen werden ohne do gebildet, wenn who dem deutschen „wer" entspricht.
who-Fragen werden mit do gebildet, wenn who dem deutschen „wen" (oder „wem") entspricht.

|  | Sandra | informs | the boss. |  |  |
|---|---|---|---|---|---|
|  | Who | informs | the boss? | – Sandra. She's the head of department. | *Wer informiert den Chef?* |
| Who does | Sandra | inform? |  | – The boss. | *Wen informiert Sandra?* |

who = „wer" bezeichnet das Subjekt des Satzes – die Person, die etwas tut.
who = „wen" bezeichnet das Objekt des Satzes – die Person, der etwas geschieht.

■ Fragen mit what, which, whose und how much/many werden ohne do gebildet, wenn das Fragewort Subjekt (oder Teil des Subjekts) ist, dagegen mit do, wenn das Fragewort Objekt (oder Teil des Objekts) ist.

| | |
|---|---|
| *What* **happened** yesterday? | *Was ist gestern passiert?* |
| What **did *you* do** yesterday? | *Was haben Sie gestern gemacht?* |
| *Which* hotel **cost** most? | *Welches Hotel kostete am meisten?* |
| Which hotel **did *you* book**? | *Welches Hotel haben Sie gebucht?* |
| *Whose* advice **seems** best? | *Wessen Rat scheint am besten zu sein?* |
| Whose advice **did *you* take**? | *Wessen Rat sind Sie gefolgt?* |
| *How many* customers **buy** our products? | *Wie viele Kunden/Kundinnen kaufen unsere Produkte?* |
| How many products **did *they* buy**? | *Wie viele Produkte kauften sie?* |

### Fragen mit Präpositionen

■ In diesen Fragen entspricht who ... with? dem deutschen „mit wem", who ... to? dem deutschen „wem".

|  |  |  |  |  |  |  |  |
|---|---|---|---|---|---|---|---|
|  | Anja had | lunch with Tom | last week. |  | He introduced | her to | his colleagues. |
| Who did | Anja **have** | lunch **with**? |  | Who did | he **introduce** | her **to**? |  |
| *Mit wem hat Anja zu Mittag gegessen?* |  |  |  | *Wem hat er sie vorgestellt?* |  |  |  |

Die Präposition (hier: with, to) steht normalerweise dort, wo sie auch sonst steht: hinter dem Verb und ggf. dessen Objekt – nicht, wie im Deutschen, vor dem Fragewort.

■ Diese Stellung der Präposition gilt auch in anderen Fragen.

|  |  |  |  |  |
|---|---|---|---|---|
|  | Max is looking for | a new job. |  | Esmeralda comes from Columbia. |
| What | **is** Max **looking for**? |  | Where does | Esmeralda **come from**? |

### Das Wichtigste in Kürze

■ who? = „wen?/wem?": Frage mit do bilden
■ Präpositionen stehen in Fragen am Ende, nicht vor dem Fragewort

Weitere Informationen ⟶ Units 26, 28

**A** **Underline the correct form.**
1 Why did you ask Peter? / Why asked you Peter?
2 Which airline do you like best? / like you best?
3 With who did you speak? / Who did you speak with?
4 Why did the deal fall through? What did happen? / What happened?
5 Who did phone just now? / Who phoned just now?
6 How much money did you spend? / spent you?
7 At what are you all looking? / What are you all looking at?

**B** **Make questions for these answers.**
1 When / the crash / happen? – It happened in the autumn of 2008.

...................................................................................................................

2 How many people / come to your presentation last week? – About fifty.

...................................................................................................................

3 What colour / go / best with this carpet? – Beige, I think.

...................................................................................................................

4 Who / help you / with your flyer? – Nobody, I designed it myself!

...................................................................................................................

5 What / normally happen / at Christmas in your office? – We usually all go out for dinner.

...................................................................................................................

6 Who / Roswitha / share an office / with? – Markus and Karin, but they don't get on very well.

...................................................................................................................

**C** **Make questions for these answers.**
A: *What did you do yesterday evening?*
B: I went out for a meal in the old town.

1 A: Who ...........................................?
   B: I went with Tomas.

2 A: Who ...........................................?
   B: He paid for the food, and I paid for the drinks.

3 A: What ...........................................?
   B: Well, we didn't talk about work.

4 A: What ........................................... after the meal?
   B: We met up with some other colleagues and went for a drink.

5 A: How many ........................................... in the group altogether?
   B: There were six of us.

6 A: Where ...........................................?
   B: To a bar.

7 A: Who ...........................................?
   B: I talked to Martina most of the time. She's very nice.

8 A: How much ...........................................?
   B: Far too much! I have a headache this morning.

**D** **Translate the following questions.**
1 Was ist passiert und wie ist es passiert?
2 Wer hat heute Morgen so früh angerufen?
3 Mit wem ist Herr Sanders nach Paris geflogen?
4 Wer hat diese Postkarte geschickt?
5 Mr Li hat die Mitteilung nicht bekommen.
   Wem haben Sie sie geschickt?

I expect you're ready for a cup of coffee, ~~no~~? **aren't you?**

You take sugar, ~~yes~~? **don't you?**

## Form

■ Frageanhängsel (oder „Bestätigungsfragen") entsprechen „nicht wahr?" bzw. „oder?" im Deutschen. Sie werden durch Wiederholung eines Hilfsverbs gebildet.

You**'re** learning Spanish, **aren't** you?     She **must** be Italian, **mustn't** she?

You **don't** know Mr Li, **do** you?     They **didn't** go by car, **did** they?

Ron **doesn't** play tennis, **does** he?     Tom **can't** speak Chinese, **can** he?

Sandra **has** been to China before, **hasn't** she?     It **won't** be cold in Milan in May, **will** it?

Ein bejahtes Hilfsverb (z. B. has) wird verneint ans Satzende gestellt (hasn't). Ein verneintes Hilfsverb (z. B. won't) wird bejaht ans Satzende gestellt (will).

■ Wie in anderen Fragen muss man eine Form von do einsetzen, wenn sonst kein Hilfsverb vorhanden ist.

You **work** hard, **don't** you?     They **flew**, **didn't** they?     Bernd **looks** after the website, **doesn't** he?

■ In einem Satz mit dem Vollverb have steht in aller Regel ein Frageanhängsel mit do, in einem Satz mit have got jedoch mit have.

You **have** a meeting every Monday, **don't** you?     Jennifer **has got** two children, **hasn't** she?

■ Beachten Sie noch diese zwei Ausnahmen.

1. I **am** late, **aren't** I (~~amn't I~~)?     2. **Let's** (= Let us) go, **shall we**?

## Intonation und Gebrauch

You like working here, **don't you?**

I've got $30. The taxi won't cost more, **will it?**

Geht die Stimme am Satzende hoch, bedeutet dies: „Ich bin mir nicht sicher. Sage mir, ob es wahr ist."

Tom doesn't really speak Arabic, **does he?**

Manchmal wird damit Überraschung ausgedrückt: „Das überrascht mich. Ist es wirklich wahr?"

Ann drives a VW, **doesn't she?** She's got a Golf.

You don't need me, **do you?** I can see that you have lots of help already.

Geht die Stimme nach unten, bedeutet dies: „Ich weiß es eigentlich. Bestätige mir, dass ich recht habe."

## Das Wichtigste in Kürze

■ Frageanhängsel sind spiegelbildlich: bejahter Satz – verneintes Anhängsel (und umgekehrt)
■ Hilfsverb im Satz vorhanden: Hilfsverb im Anhängsel wiederholen
■ Kein Hilfsverb im Satz vorhanden: Frageanhängsel mit einer Form von do

Weitere Informationen → Units 26, 27

**A** **Underline the correct form.**
1  You live near here, **aren't you?** / **don't you?**
2  You won't be late, **will you?** / **won't you?**
3  You don't mind if I'm not there, **are you?** / **do you?**
4  I'm the last, **am not I?** / **aren't I?**
5  She's been very busy lately, **hasn't she?** / **isn't she?**
6  We've got enough time, **don't we?** / **haven't we?**

**B** **Add question tags.**
1  I've told you about my meeting with the Koreans, .............................?
2  It's much nicer in the new building, .............................?
3  You don't really expect him to phone, .............................?
4  You work with Frau Mertens, .............................?
5  Sandra worked with Max Klein before, .............................?
6  I'm asking too many questions, .............................?
7  You're not very pleased about the changes, .............................?
8  You always stay at the Monkton Hotel, .............................?
9  Mike had a meeting with the Thai supplier, .............................?

**C** **Make questions with question tags for these answers.**
A: You didn't stay at home yesterday, did you?
B: No, of course I didn't stay at home. I went to Jane's party.

1  A: You ............................. all last weekend, .................................?
B: Yes, I worked both Saturday and Sunday.
2  A: You ................................. with the way I handled the situation, ...........................?
B: No, I'm not very happy. I think you could have been more careful.
3  A: Jackie ............................. a new job, .............................?
B: Yes, she has. She found it through a friend.
4  A: Prices ............................. again, .............................?
B: Yes, they are. They've risen every month this year and don't look as though they're going to stop.
5  A: You ......................... upset if I don't come to your farewell party, ...........................?
B: No, of course I won't. I know you're going to be away.
6  A: Ms Watson's grandfather ............................. the company, .............................?
B: Yes, that's right. He founded it in 1954.

**D** **Translate the following questions.**
1  Sie kommen morgen, oder, Herr Henderson?
2  Das war sehr teuer, nicht wahr?
3  John hat gestern nicht angerufen, oder?
4  Sie arbeiten hier schon lange, oder?
5  Der Besitzer verlor viel Geld, nicht wahr?

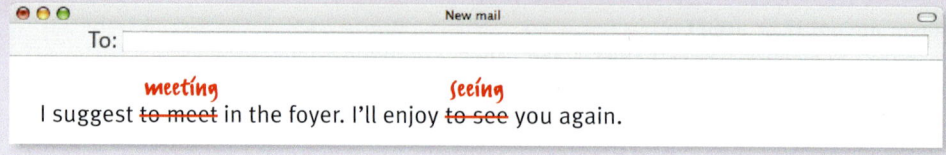

I suggest ~~to meet~~ **meeting** in the foyer. I'll enjoy ~~to see~~ **seeing** you again.

## Definition des Gerundiums

■ Ein Gerundium ist eine Mischung aus Verb und Nomen. Es ist von einem Verb abgeleitet und identisch mit dessen **-ing**-Form. Es funktioniert jedoch wie ein Nomen und kann zum Beispiel Subjekt eines Satzes sein.
You can't smoke here. **Smoking** is not allowed. *(Das) Rauchen ist hier nicht gestattet.*

## Gerundium nach bestimmten Verben

■ Das Gerundium steht als Objekt nach bestimmten Verben. Oft entspricht es einem Infinitiv im Deutschen.
Can you **imagine working** (~~to work~~) at night? *Kannst du dir vorstellen, nachts zu arbeiten?*
We **risk losing** (~~to lose~~) all our investment. *Wir riskieren, unsere gesamte Investition zu verlieren.*
I **suggest going** (~~to go~~) by train. *Ich schlage vor, mit dem Zug zu fahren.*
They **recommend booking** (~~to book~~) early. *Sie empfehlen, früh zu buchen.*
I **can't help seeing** the parallels with last year. *Ich kann nicht umhin, die Parallelen ... zu sehen.*
Do you **mind waiting** (~~to wait~~)? *Macht es Ihnen etwas aus zu warten?*

■ Verb + *...ing* wird z. T. im Deutschen auch anders wiedergegeben.
I **like travelling**. *Ich reise gern.*
They **kept (on)** / **carried on asking** questions. *Sie stellten immer wieder Fragen.*
The plan **will involve relocating** some departments. *Der Plan wird mit sich bringen, dass ... verlegt werden.*
She **mentioned meeting** Mr Li in Frankfurt. *Sie erwähnte, dass sie Mr Li in Frankfurt getroffen hat/habe.*
They've **postponed disbanding** the service team. *Sie haben die Auflösung des Serviceteams verschoben.*
Have you **finished photocopying**? *Sind Sie mit dem Fotokopieren fertig?*

■ Zu den Verben, auf die ein Gerundium folgt, zählen insbesondere folgende:

| Verben des Mögens und Nichtmögens | Verbens des Beginnens, Fortsetzens und Beendens | Sonstige Verben |
|---|---|---|
| | | **admit** *zugeben* |
| **like*** *gern haben/tun* | **start*** *anfangen* | **avoid** *vermeiden* |
| **love*** *sehr gern haben/tun* | **begin*** *beginnen* | **can't help** *nicht umhinkönnen* |
| **enjoy** *gern haben/tun* | **continue** *weiter tun* | **consider** *erwägen* |
| **dislike** *ungern haben/tun* | **carry on** / **go on** *weiter tun* | **imagine** *sich vorstellen* |
| **hate*** *sehr ungern haben/tun* | **keep (on)** *weiter tun* | **involve** *mit sich bringen* |
| **prefer*** *lieber haben/tun* | **finish** *zu Ende machen* | **mention** *erwähnen* |
| **(not) mind** *etwas/nichts dagegen haben* | **stop** *aufhören* | **miss** *vermissen* |
| | **give up** *aufgeben* | **recommend** *empfehlen* |
| | **postpone** *aufschieben* | **suggest** *vorschlagen* |

Auf die mit * gekennzeichneten Verben (in dieser Bedeutung) kann auch ein Infinitiv folgen.

**!** Auf **would like** *(möchte/n)*, **would love** *(würde/n liebend gern)*, **would prefer** *(würde/n lieber)*, **would hate** *(würde/n sehr ungern)* folgt immer ein **to**-Infinitiv.
**I'd like to ask** (~~asking~~) a question. *Ich möchte eine Frage stellen.*

■ Auf viele andere Verben folgt ebenfalls – wie im Deutschen – immer ein Infinitiv, z. B. **afford** *(sich leisten)*, **agree**, **decide**, **expect**, **manage** *(es schaffen)*, **offer**, **plan**, **promise**, **refuse** *(sich weigern)*, **seem**, **want**.

## Das Wichtigste in Kürze

■ *...ing* nach bestimmten Verben, insbesondere Verben des Mögens und Nicht-Mögens und Verben, die Beginnen, Fortsetzen und Beenden ausdrücken

**A** **Underline the correct form.**

1 We've postponed **meeting** / **to meet** till next week.
2 I've suggested **to wait** / **waiting** for the new figures that we'll get next Monday.
3 They'd like **expanding** / **to expand** their business in Russia.
4 I can't imagine **have to work** / **having to work** under Brian Tomkins.
5 We can't afford **paying** / **to pay** them any more.
6 Jan's new job will involve **moving** / **to move** to Berlin.

**B** **Rewrite these sentences using the gerund.**

1 Herbert said, "We can eat in the hotel." Herbert suggested ................................................

2 Ann said, "It would be nice to live in Hong Kong." Ann said she could imagine ............................

3 Mr Li said, "You should book the hotel early." Mr Li recommended ..........................................

4 Bernd asked, "Would you wait for me?" Bernd asked if I would mind ......................................

5 Mark said, "I might apply for the job." Mark is considering ................................................

**C** **Complete these dialogues using the gerund or the infinitive.**

1 A: Ron has suggested .................... (stay) in a motel further away from the exhibition centre.

   B: I don't want .................... (be) so far out of town. I'd prefer .................... (stay) in our
   usual hotel, even if it's more expensive.

2 A: Would you mind .................... (tell) me what is going on?

   B: They are planning .................... (close down) the production department and are considering
   .................... (move) it to the Czech Republic.

3 A: I think we should leave early tomorrow to avoid .................... (drive) in the rush hour.

   B: You know I hate .................... (get up) early. I'd like .................... (go) later.

4 A: We can't afford .................... (wait) until next week, so we've decided ....................
   (make) an announcement tomorrow.

   B: Can't you postpone .................... (make) it at least till Friday? I can't help ....................
   (think) that an announcement now will cause more problems.

5 A: I can't imagine .................... (work) in an international team. How have you found it?

   B: Well it involves .................... (be) very flexible and cooperative, but we've all managed
   .................... (adapt), and I'd like .................... (think) that it's a great success.

6 A: I'm going to miss .................... (have) you as a colleague. Actually, I'd love ....................
   (come) with you to France. Don't they need someone like me in sunny Marseilles too?

   B: They might. I'd recommend .................... (have) a discreet word with Paul Malraux.

**D** **Translate the following sentences.**

1 Ich schlage vor, Mr Li und seine Kollegen hier nach Deutschland einzuladen.
2 Kathrin hat angeboten, mir bei [mit] der Präsentation zu helfen.
3 Viele Japaner können sich nicht vorstellen, ihre Firma zu verlassen und bei einer anderen zu arbeiten.
4 Macht es Ihnen etwas aus, mit der U-Bahn zu fahren? Das ist schneller als mit dem Taxi.

# 30 Gerund (2): Preposition + ...ing
## Gerundium (2): Präposition + ...*ing*

I'm afraid my colleague changed the time of the meeting without ~~to tell~~ telling me.

**Präposition + Gerundium**

- **Auf eine Präposition (about, against, at, for, in, of, on, without usw.) folgt ein Gerundium. Die Präposition kann allein stehen oder mit einem Adjektiv, Nomen oder Verb eine Einheit bilden. Zu den allein stehenden Präpositionen zählen: before, after, for, against, instead of, like, than, without, by** *(indem)*.
  **Before making** a decision, we should ask Maria. *Bevor wir eine Entscheidung fällen, ...*
  I'm **for/against outsourcing** production. *Ich bin dafür/dagegen, die Produktion auszugliedern.*
  **Instead of emailing**, I phoned. *Anstatt zu mailen, habe ich angerufen.*
  Investing in shares is **like playing** poker. *In Aktien zu investieren, ist wie Poker spielen.*
  Is a personal phone call better **than sending** an email? *... besser als eine E-Mail zu schicken?*
  She left the company **without saying** goodbye. *Sie verließ die Firma, ohne sich zu verabschieden.*
  You save money **by booking** through an agency. *Man spart Geld, indem man über eine Agentur bucht.*

- Adjektiv + Präposition + Gerundium
  I was **afraid of making** a mistake. *Ich hatte Angst, einen Fehler zu machen.*
  He's very **good/bad at delegating**. *Er ist gut/schlecht im Delegieren.*
  I'm **responsible for informing** the boss. *Ich bin dafür verantwortlich, die Chefin zu informieren.*
  I'm **tired of / fed up with working** at weekends. *Ich habe es satt, am Wochenende zu arbeiten.*

- Nomen + Präposition + Gerundium
  Do you have any **experience of leading** a team? *Haben Sie Erfahrung darin, ein Team zu leiten?*
  What are the **chances of finding** a taxi? *Wie stehen die Chancen, ein Taxi zu finden?*
  What will be the **effect of raising** the price? *Welche Wirkung wird es haben, den Preis zu erhöhen?*
  I hate the **idea/thought of paying** so much. *Ich hasse die Idee / den Gedanken, so viel zu bezahlen.*
  There's a **danger/risk of losing** our investment. *Es besteht die Gefahr / das Risiko, ... zu verlieren.*
  There's no **excuse for making** mistakes. *Es gibt keine Entschuldigung dafür, Fehler zu machen.*
  There are good **reasons for making** the change. *Es gibt gute Gründe dafür, die Änderung durchzuführen.*
  I had no **difficulty/trouble (in) finding** a hotel. *Ich hatte keine Schwierigkeiten/Mühe, ein Hotel zu finden.*

- Verb + Präposition + Gerundium
  He **talked/spoke about/of going** abroad. *Er sprach davon, ins Ausland zu gehen.*
  I often **dream about/of setting** up my own business. *Ich träume oft davon, eine eigene Firma zu gründen.*
  **I'm thinking about/of applying** for the post. *Ich überlege, mich für den Posten zu bewerben.*
  I **apologized for being** late. *Ich entschuldigte mich dafür, dass ich zu spät kam.*
  We **are concentrating on cutting** costs. *Wir konzentrieren uns darauf, Kosten zu senken.*
  We **succeeded in persuading** her. *Es gelang uns, sie zu überzeugen.*
  **Do** you **worry about making** mistakes? *Machen Sie sich Sorgen, dass Sie Fehler machen könnten?*
  Success **will depend on finding** a good partner. *Der Erfolg wird davon abhängen, ... zu finden.*
  He **insisted on showing** me his photos. *Er bestand darauf, mir seine Fotos zu zeigen.*

- **Zwischen Verb und Präposition kann auch ein Objekt (eine Person oder Sache) stehen.**
  She **thanked us for helping** her. *Sie dankte uns dafür, dass wir ihr geholfen hatten.*
  He **blamed me for losing** the contract. *Er gab mir die Schuld, dass wir den Auftrag verloren hatten.*
  I **criticized them for being** so naive. *Ich kritisierte sie dafür, dass sie so naiv gewesen sind.*

**Das Wichtigste in Kürze**

- Nach einer Präposition: *-ing*-Form, nicht Infinitiv!



Weitere Informationen → Units 29, 31–33

**A** Underline the correct form.

1 I'm not **interested for going** / **interested in going** on that training course they're offering.
2 Are you **good at making** / **good in making** quick decisions?
3 They decided everything without **letting** / **to let** me know.
4 Business ethics in that country are terrible. It's like **doing** / **to do** business with the mafia!
5 I'm very much for **involving** / **to involve** the whole team in important decisions.
6 Did you have any **difficulty in getting** / **difficulty on getting** a visa?

**B** Rewrite these sentences with the preposition + gerund.

1 I left. I didn't see any of the sights. **(without)** I left without ..................................................

2 We didn't fly. We went by train. **(instead of)** Instead of ....................................................

3 Tom informed his colleagues, then cleared his desk and left within an hour. **(after)**

 ............................................................................................................

4 We can save 10% if we buy from the company in Lithuania. **(by)**

 ............................................................................................................

 **In these sentences you have to decide which preposition is needed.**

5 I'd like to meet your new boss. ⋯⟩ I'm interested ....................................................

6 I'm tired of doing Donald's work for him. ⋯⟩ I'm fed up ....................................................

7 They've managed to find offices. ⋯⟩ They've succeeded ....................................................

8 I didn't want John to help me, but he did. ⋯⟩ John insisted ....................................................

**C** Complete the dialogues with the correct preposition and gerund.

1 A: The chances ........................ **(get)** well-qualified people is quite good in this economic climate.

 B: We want someone who has experience ........................ **(manage)** a large customer base.

2 A: You're usually good ........................ **(remember)** names. What's the name of that restaurant we

 took Mr Li to last month? I'm thinking ........................ **(book)** a table for tomorrow night. I'm

 responsible ........................ **(entertain)** the team from our Swedish partner.

 B: I'm sorry, but I've forgotten. But there'll be no difficulty ........................ **(find)** out.

3 A: When you don't use a language for a while there's always a risk ........................ **(forget)** what

 you've learned. I always worry ........................ **(make)** mistakes and have to remind myself that

 the important thing is to concentrate ........................ **(get)** the message across.

 B: Absolutely. It's silly to criticize people ........................ **(not be)** perfect.

**D** Translate the following sentences using the gerund and, where necessary, the correct preposition.

1 Kerstin entschuldigte sich dafür, dass sie nicht genug Kopien gemacht hatte.
2 Magda kann komplizierte Sachen gut erklären.
3 Es gelang uns, die Kosten zu reduzieren.
4 Der Gedanke, die Arbeitsstelle zu verlieren, ist immer schlimm.
5 Wie können sie Kosten senken *(reduce)*, ohne Leute zu entlassen *(make redundant)*?
6 Anstatt zu warten, bis sie uns kontaktieren, sollten wir ein Angebot machen.
7 Matthias versteht das neue System nicht und überlegt *(consider)*, Ramona um Hilfe zu bitten.

**New mail**

To:

I'm looking forward ~~to see~~ *to seeing* you again. How about ~~to go~~ *going* out to dinner together one evening?

### to + Gerundium

- Normalerweise ist to Teil des Infinitivs. In bestimmten Fällen ist to jedoch Präposition und Teil einer Wendung, auf die ein Gerundium folgt.

  We **are looking forward to meeting** (~~meet~~) Mr Li. *Wir freuen uns darauf, Mr Li kennen zu lernen.*

  I'm **used to waiting** (~~wait~~) for decisions. *Ich bin es gewohnt, auf Entscheidungen zu warten.*

  Ed never **got used to working** (~~work~~) under Mr Lee. *Ed hat sich nie daran gewöhnt, unter ... zu arbeiten.*

  **Does** anyone **object to trying** (~~try~~) a new design studio? *Hat jemand etwas dagegen, ... auszuprobieren?*

  Auf **used to** kann auch, in ganz anderer Bedeutung, ein Infinitiv folgen. Beachten Sie den Unterschied.

  I **used to commute** by train. *Früher bin ich (immer) mit dem Zug gependelt.*

  I'm **used to commuting** by train. *Ich bin es gewohnt, mit dem Zug zu pendeln.*

### Wendungen + Gerundium

- Auch nach einigen idiomatischen Wendungen steht ein Gerundium.

  **How/What about going** out for a drink this evening? *Wie wäre es, wenn wir ... etwas trinken gehen?*

  It's **not worth waiting** any longer. *Es lohnt sich nicht, länger zu warten.*

  I **don't feel like going** out this evening. *Ich habe keine Lust, heute Abend wegzugehen.*

  **What's the point of paying** more? *Welchen Sinn hat es, mehr zu bezahlen?*

  **There's no/little point in asking** Rod for help. *Es hat keinen/wenig Sinn, Rod um Hilfe zu bitten.*

  It's **no good/use worrying**. *Es bringt nichts, sich Sorgen zu machen.*

### Gerundium mit eigenem Subjekt

- In vielen Fällen kann vor dem Gerundium auch ein Nomen oder Pronomen stehen. Dieses ist Subjekt des Gerundiums, hat jedoch als Pronomen die Objektform! Im Deutschen gibt es keine genaue Entsprechung.

  Mike is difficult. He **hates me giving** him instructions. *... Er hasst es, wenn ich ihm Anweisungen erteile.*

  How can we do this **without someone finding** out? *Wie können wir dies tun, ohne dass jemand es erfährt?*

  **There's no chance of us meeting** this deadline. *Es besteht keine Chance, dass wir den Termin schaffen.*

  **There's no point in me talking** to the boss. *Es hat keinen Sinn, dass ich mit der Chefin spreche.*

### Passivform des Gerundiums

- Die Passivform des Gerundiums ist being + Partizip Perfekt.

  Everyone likes **being praised**. *Jeder hat es gern, gelobt zu werden.*

  I'm afraid of **being overtaken** by younger colleagues. *Ich habe Angst davor, von ... überholt zu werden.*

  Tina objected to **being moved**. *Tina protestierte dagegen, versetzt zu werden.*

### Gerundium + Infinitiv

- Manchmal handelt es sich beim Gerundium um ein Verb, das mit einem Infinitiv weiter verbunden wird.

  We**'re used to having to make** last-minute changes.

  *Wir sind es gewöhnt, Veränderungen in letzter Minute machen zu müssen.*

### Das Wichtigste in Kürze

- Gerundium nach to in bestimmten Fällen: look forward to, be/get used to, object to
- Gerundium nach idiomatischen Wendungen wie: how/what about?, it's worth, feel like, it's no good/use
- Gerundium mit eigenem Subjekt: Pronomen in der Objektform
- Passivform des Gerundiums: being + Partizip Perfekt

Weitere Informationen → Units 29, 30, 32, 33

**A** **Underline the correct form.**

1 In Europe we're not used to **eating** / **eat** with our fingers in a restaurant.
2 What's the point **of waiting** / **to wait** any longer?
3 I am looking forward to **work** / **working** together.
4 Maxine used to **work** / **working** for a Japanese company before coming here.
5 It's not worth **consulting** / **to consult** the so-called experts. We have to decide ourselves.

**B** **Rewrite these sentences using the gerund.**

1 Max doesn't mind working on Saturdays. ⇢ Max is used ...................................................

2 I hate to tell customers lies. ⇢ I object ...................................................

3 Would you like to join us for lunch? ⇢ Do you feel ...................................................

4 It's not a good idea to buy the insurance. ⇢ It's not worth ...................................................

5 There is no reason why we should continue. ⇢ There's no point in ...................................................

6 Why don't we take our guests to a beer garden? ⇢ How about ...................................................

7 Do you want to move to the Vienna office? ⇢ Are you looking forward ...................................................

**C** **Rewrite these sentences as in the example.**
There's no chance. **They** won't accept these terms.
There's no chance of them accepting these terms.

1 I can't make any phone calls. **My colleagues** listen all the time.

   I can't make any phone calls without ...................................................

2 **Julia and I** make the coffee every morning. Why don't you do it for a change?

   Instead of ................................................... why don't you do it for a change?

3 **People** look over my shoulder when I'm working. I don't like it.

   I dislike ................................................... when I'm working.

4 How likely is it that **we** will get the contract?

   What are the chances ...................................................

5 How can we do market research? **The competition** will find out about our plans.

   How can we do market research without ...................................................

**D** **Complete these sentences with a preposition where needed and a passive gerund.**

1 I don't mind ..................... (give) advice, but I don't like ....................... (tell) what to do.

2 In the Christmas period we are all used ........................... (ask) to do overtime at short notice.

3 Max insists ........................... (inform) about the smallest details.

4 You can't be a press officer if you're afraid ........................... (grill) by journalists.

**E** **Translate the following sentences.**

1 Ich hasse es, am Wochenende arbeiten zu müssen.
2 Es hat keinen Sinn, mich zu fragen. Ich weiß nichts.
3 Wir freuen uns, Sie und Ihr Team nächste Woche zu sehen.
4 Ich bin gewohnt, bis spät in den Abend zu arbeiten.
5 Es lohnt sich immer, einen Experten im Team zu haben.

> to spend
> We can't afford ~~spending~~ any more time or money on this issue.

## Verb + Infinitiv

- Wie in Unit 29 erwähnt, folgt auf viele Verben, wie im Deutschen, immer ein Infinitiv. Dazu gehören u. a.:

**afford** *es sich leisten*     **expect** *damit rechnen*     **offer** *anbieten*     **seem** *scheinen*
**agree** *sich einigen*     **hope** *hoffen*     **plan** *planen*     **try** *versuchen*
**decide** *beschließen,*     **learn** *lernen*     **promise** *versprechen*     **want** *wollen*
  *sich entscheiden*     **manage** *es schaffen*     **refuse** *sich weigern*

We can't **afford to wait** any longer. *Wir können es uns nicht leisten, länger zu warten.*
He just **refused to listen** to me. *Er hat sich schlicht geweigert, mir zuzuhören.*
I **managed to persuade** them to accept the lower price. *Mir ist es gelungen, / Ich habe es geschafft, sie zu überreden, den niedrigeren Preis zu akzeptieren.*

## Verb + Gerundium oder Infinitiv

- Wie in Unit 29 ebenfalls ausgeführt, folgt auf einige Verben ohne Bedeutungsunterschied ein Infinitiv oder ein Gerundium: **begin, start, like, love, hate, prefer, intend** *(beabsichtigen)*.
  People in the audience **started to yawn** / **started yawning**. *Zuhörer fingen an zu gähnen.*
  I **prefer to commute** / **commuting** by train. *Ich ziehe es vor, mit dem Zug zu pendeln.*
  We **intend to build** / **building** a new factory. *Wir haben vor, eine neue Fabrik zu bauen.*

- Bei einigen Verben ergibt sich jedoch ein Bedeutungsunterschied.
  I must **remember to phone** Vladimir. *Ich muss daran denken, Vladimir anzurufen.*
  I **remember meeting** Vladimir in Moscow two years ago. *Ich erinnere mich daran, wie ich Vladimir ... traf.*

  I mustn't **forget to phone** New York. *Ich darf nicht vergessen, in New York anzurufen.*
  I'll never **forget arriving** in New York. *Ich werde nie vergessen, wie ich in New York ankam.*

  The presenter **stopped to answer** a question. *Der Vortragende hielt an / unterbrach, um ... zu beantworten.*
  He **stopped giving** presentations last year. *Er hat letztes Jahr aufgehört, Präsentationen zu machen.*

  I **meant to tell** you, but I forgot. *Ich wollte / hatte vor, es Ihnen zu sagen, aber ich habe es vergessen.*
  This **means having** to postpone the launch. *Dies bedeutet, dass wir die Produkteinführung verschieben müssen.*

  I **regret to have to** tell you that Mr Sams is no longer with us. *Ich muss Ihnen leider mitteilen, dass ...*
  I **have** never **regretted changing** my job. *Ich habe nie bedauert, dass ich ... gewechselt habe.*

  I **tried to convince** my boss, but he wouldn't change his mind.
  *Ich habe versucht, meinen Chef zu überzeugen, aber er wollte seine Meinung nicht ändern.*
  We **tried reducing** the price, but that didn't increase sales.
  *Wir haben ausprobiert, den Preis zu reduzieren, aber das erhöhte die Verkäufe nicht.*

## Das Wichtigste in Kürze

- Infinitiv oder Gerundium möglich:
  ohne Bedeutungsunterschied: nach **begin, start, like, love, hate, prefer, intend**
  mit Bedeutungsunterschied: nach **remember, forget, stop, mean, regret, try**

Weitere Informationen → Units 29, 33

**A** **Underline the correct form.**

1 Did you remember **sending** / **to send** Martin the missing document?
2 The flight is at 6.40 in the morning. That means **to get up** / **getting up** very early.
3 They've agreed **giving** / **to give** us a 10% discount.
4 Can we afford **paying** / **to pay** for TV advertising?
5 When I went to Mexico City for the first time, I remember **being** / **to be** totally confused.
6 We regret **informing** / **to inform** you that the model you wish to order is no longer available.
7 The satnav broke down so we had to stop **asking** / **to ask** someone the way.

**B** **Complete the second sentence so that it has the same meaning as the first.**

1 Pete planned to phone you, but he forgot.

Pete meant ...............................................................................................................

2 I interrupted the interview and made a phone call.

I stopped ...............................................................................................................

3 Once I went to Mumbai. I'll never forget it.

I'll never forget ...............................................................................................................

4 I'm sure I saw the file on Roland's desk.

I remember ...............................................................................................................

5 Have you given up smoking?

Have you stopped ...............................................................................................................

6 I was very ill after I ate some fish. It was terrible.

I'll never forget ...............................................................................................................

**C** **Complete the dialogues with the gerund or the infinitive. Add a preposition where necessary.**

1 A: Where is the key? I remember ..................... **(put)** it on the table.

B: Here it is. I suggest ..................... **(leave)** it in the conference room door in future.

2 A: I meant ..................... **(tell)** you about that calendar the Russian company sent at Christmas.

B: I saw it. I'd never dream ..................... **(use)** photos like that in a business calendar.

3 A: Is it worth ..................... **(ask)** Michelle if we can have a bit more time to finish this?

B: No, I've stopped ..................... **(ask)** questions like that. She always says no.

4 A: I regret ..................... **(say)** that we can't afford ..................... **(provide)** a free service
   any more.

B: Does that mean ..................... **(ask)** people to pay for it? Or do you want to stop the service
   altogether?

5 A: Both sides have agreed ..................... **(meet)** again on Thursday.

B: So there's a chance ..................... **(get)** an agreement before the end of the week.

**D** **Translate the following sentences.**

1 Ich muss daran denken, Marketing zu informieren.
2 Wir haben aufgehört, nach neuen Büroräumen zu suchen.
3 Wo ist der Beamer? Ich erinnere mich daran, dass ich ihn an die Exportabteilung ausgeliehen habe.
4 Ich kann mir nicht leisten, mehr Zeit in dieses Projekt zu investieren.
5 Adriane weigert sich, mit Stefan zusammenzuarbeiten.

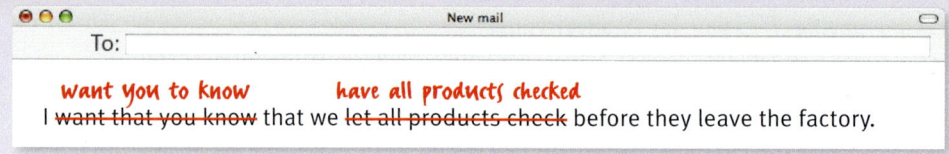

**want you to know**      **have all products checked**

I ~~want that you know~~ that we ~~let all products check~~ before they leave the factory.

### Verb + Objekt + **to**-Infinitiv mit Parallelkonstruktion im Deutschen

- Auf bestimmte Verben folgt ein Objekt + Infinitiv. Oft ist die Konstruktion im Deutschen ähnlich.
  I **asked David to help** me. *Ich bat David, mir zu helfen.*
  She **told me to clear** my desk. *Sie forderte mich auf, meinen Schreibtisch zu räumen.*

| | | | |
|---|---|---|---|
| **advise** *raten* | **force** *zwingen* | **order** *befehlen* | **tell** *auffordern* |
| **allow** *erlauben* | **help** *helfen* | **persuade** *überreden* | **warn** *warnen; ermahnen* |
| **ask** *bitten* | **invite** *einladen* | **remind** *erinnern* | |

**warn** verwendet man mit **not**, wenn ausgedrückt wird, dass jemand etwas nicht machen soll.
I **warned them not to pay** in advance. *Ich warnte sie davor, im Voraus zu bezahlen.*

### Sonderfall Deutsch „lassen"

- Je nach Bedeutung drückt man „jemanden etwas machen lassen" im Englischen unterschiedlich aus.
  Der Infinitiv steht dabei nach **let**, **make** und **have** ohne **to**, nach **get** mit **to**.

  jdn. etwas machen lassen = jdm. erlauben etwas zu tun: **let sb. do sth.**
  **Let me explain** the plan. *Lassen Sie mich das Vorhaben erklären.*

  jdn. etwas machen lassen = jdn. dazu bringen/zwingen etwas zu tun: **make sb. do sth.**
  His questions **made me hesitate**. *Seine Fragen ließen mich zögern.*
  He **made me wait** a whole hour. *Er ließ mich eine ganze Stunde warten.*

  jdn. etwas machen lassen = veranlassen, dass jd. etwas tut: **have sb. do sth.** / **get sb. to do sth.**
  I'll **have Max drive** you. / I'll **get Max to drive** you to the airport. *Ich lasse Max Sie zum Flughafen fahren.*

  Die Passivform von **have sb. do sth.** heißt **have sth. done.**
  I'm **having copies made**. *Ich lasse (gerade) Kopien machen.*
  We **have the flyers printed** in Italy. *Wir lassen die Flyer in Italien drucken.*

### Verb + Objekt + Infinitiv ohne Parallelkonstruktion im Deutschen

Bei einigen Verben, insbesondere Verben des Wollens und Nicht-Wollens, entspricht ein Objekt + Infinitiv einem deutschen Satz mit „dass/wenn".
I **want you to inform** the staff (~~want that you inform the staff~~). *Ich will, dass Sie die Belegschaft informieren.*
I **would like you to stay** for dinner (~~would like that ...~~). *Ich möchte, dass Sie zum Essen bleiben.*
I **would prefer them to find** a different solution. *Ich hätte es lieber, wenn sie eine andere Lösung fänden.*
I **would hate Alice to quit** (~~would hate that ...~~). *Ich hätte es sehr ungern, wenn Alice kündigen würde.*
We **are waiting for the speaker to finish** (~~waiting that ...~~). *Wir warten darauf, dass der Sprecher zu Ende kommt.*

Ein **that**-Satz ist nach diesen Verben im Englischen **nicht** möglich.

Nach **expect** hängt es von der Bedeutung ab, ob ein **that**-Satz angeschlossen werden kann.
I **don't expect that there will be** any problems. *Ich erwarte nicht, dass es Probleme gibt.*
I **expect you to be** on time (~~expect that ...~~). *Ich erwarte (= verlange), dass Sie pünktlich sind.*

### Das Wichtigste in Kürze

- Nach **let, make, have** (lassen): Infinitiv ohne **to**
- Nach **want, (would) like/hate/prefer, wait for**: **kein** ~~that~~-Satz

Weitere Informationen → Unit 32

**A** Underline the correct form.

1 Martin asked me **show** / **to show** him the figures again.
2 They didn't let anyone **ask** / **to ask** questions.
3 Would you like **me to help** / **that I help** you?
4 I don't want **anyone to find out** / **that anyone finds out**.
5 Can't we get someone else **do** / **to do** this?
6 I warned you before **not to speak** / **to speak** to the press.
7 We're waiting **for the management to give** / **that the management gives** its OK.

**B** Rewrite the following sentences using the words in brackets and an infinitive.

1 A friend has asked me to become her business partner. **(would like)**
..............................................................................................
2 I think everyone should be here by nine o'clock. **(expect)**
..............................................................................................
3 My boss wouldn't allow me to take Friday off. **(let)**
..............................................................................................
4 I will make arrangements so that someone shows you round the factory. **(get)**
..............................................................................................
5 I told Emily that she shouldn't trust Brian. **(warn)**
..............................................................................................
6 Mr Smart said I had to finish everything before I went home yesterday. **(make)**
..............................................................................................
7 Can you ask someone to book a taxi for me? **(have)**
..............................................................................................
8 Ms Walters said I could borrow a company car. **(let)**
..............................................................................................
9 Sam isn't happy with our plan to reorganize the office. **(not want)**
..............................................................................................

**C** Complete the following questions.

1 A: Do you want ............................................... or can you manage on your own?
B: It's OK. I don't think I need any help, thanks.

2 A: Would you like ............................................... ?
B: Yes, please. Maja normally gives me a lift, but she's away this week of course.

3 A: Have you got enough cash or do you want ............................................... you some money?
B: Well, if you could lend me $50, that would be great.

4 A: Isn't that Frank's car? Didn't you warn ............................................... right by the entrance?
B: Yes, but he thinks it's OK to park there.

5 A: Can you remind ............................................... Ann before we go?
B: Sure. What do you need to speak to her about?

6 A: Why did Hodgson make ............................................... the report again?
B: Because he said it was all wrong.

**D** Translate the following sentences.

1 Ich warte darauf, dass jemand das Fenster repariert.
2 Wo lassen Sie die Broschüren drucken?
3 Letztes Jahr haben sie mir erlaubt, Erster Klasse zu fahren.
4 Wir lassen ein Büffet liefern.
5 Meine Chefin will, dass ich am Wochenende arbeite.
6 Wir haben ihn davor gewarnt, in diese Firma zu investieren.
7 Ich hätte gerne, dass Sie Herrn Williams begleiten.

There is something <del>what</del> **that** is causing problems and I need to speak to the person <del>which</del> **who/that** is responsible.

### Relativsätze mit who, which, that, whose

- In den folgenden Sätzen sind **who don't speak English** und **which break down all the time** Relativsätze.
  *Colleagues* **who don't speak English** have problems. *Kollegen, die kein Englisch sprechen, ...*
  *Machines* **which break down all the time** are useless. *Maschinen, die ständig kaputt gehen, sind nutzlos.*

  **Mit einem Relativsatz bestimmt man Personen oder Sachen genauer.**

- Relativsätze, die Personen genauer bestimmen, werden durch **who** oder **that** eingeleitet.
  Relativsätze, die Sachen genauer bestimmen, werden durch **which** oder **that** eingeleitet.
  Is this *the man* **who/that** stole your laptop? *Ist das der Mann, der Ihren Laptop gestohlen hat?*
  We need *a solution* **which/that** doesn't cost much. *Wir brauchen eine Lösung, die nicht viel kostet.*

  **Diese Relativsätze werden nicht durch Kommas abgetrennt.**

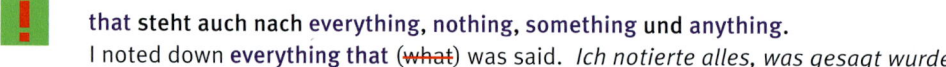 **that** steht auch nach **everything, nothing, something** und **anything**.
I noted down **everything that** (<del>what</del>) was said. *Ich notierte alles, was gesagt wurde.*

**!** Das deutsche „das, was" wird im Englischen nur mit **what** wiedergegeben.
**What** (<del>That what</del>) he showed me looked interesting. *Das, was er mir zeigte, sah interessant aus.*

- **whose** entspricht „dessen/deren".
  He's *the man* **whose** uncle founded the company. *... der Mann, dessen Onkel die Firma gegründet hat.*
  They're *the technicians* **whose** car broke down. *... die Techniker, deren Auto eine Panne hatte.*

### Relativsätze ohne Relativpronomen

- In den folgenden Sätzen ist **he** und **who** das Subjekt des Satzes (= derjenige, der arbeitet).

  Tom is a rep. **He** works for a French company.
  Tom is a rep **who** works for a French company. *... ein Vertreter, der für eine französische Firma arbeitet.*

- In den folgenden Sätzen ist **we** Subjekt des Verbs **met**; **who** ist nicht Subjekt, sondern Objekt
  (= denjenigen, den wir kennen gelernt haben).

  Tom is the rep. **We** met **him** at the fair.
  Tom is the rep **who** **we** met at the fair. *... der Vertreter, den wir auf der Messe kennen gelernt haben.*
  **Das Relativpronomen ist nicht Subjekt, sondern Objekt, wenn zwischen who/which/that und dem Verb ein Pronomen oder Nomen steht.**

- **Wenn das Relativpronomen nicht Subjekt, sondern Objekt ist, kann es weggelassen werden.**
  Tom is the rep **(who/that)** *we* met at the trade fair.
  Was Martina the woman **(who/that)** *I* saw in your office?
  I'm going to book the same hotel **(which/that)** *I* used last time.

> **Das Wichtigste in Kürze**
- Personen: **who/that** — Sachen: **which/that**
- **who/which/that** kann man weglassen, wenn ein anderes Wort Subjekt des Relativsatzes ist
- Relativsätze, die etwas/jdn. genauer bestimmen, stehen ohne Kommas!

**A** **Underline the correct form.**

1  The man  **he**  /  **who**  is working in Rainer's office is from the tax office.
2  This is the information  **they gave me**  /  **what they gave me**.
3  I can show you the website  **I usually use**  /  **what I usually use**.
4  Elena is the translator  **which**  /  **who**  is helping me in the negotiations.
5  **That what**  /  **What**  I had to do in my old job was worse than this.
6  Max is the guy  **who's**  /  **whose**  colleague was arrested by the police.
7  We need to look elsewhere. There's nothing here  **that**  /  **what**  will help us.

**B** **Put brackets ( ) round the relative pronouns which are not necessary.**

1  What happened to the coffee filters which I bought yesterday?

2  Rod and Stella are the couple whose firm nearly went bankrupt.

3  The specifications which they've given us are incomplete.

4  I've just had an email from the guy that I met on the plane to Sydney.

5  The person who agreed the contract with you has left the company.

6  The person who Maja always uses as a translator is much cheaper.

7  My boss never seems to read the emails which I send him.

**C** **Where necessary, add the missing relative pronouns.**

1  I've just checked the figures .................... Sarah got from Hong Kong.

2  What's the name of your colleague .................... husband works in Saudi Arabia?

3  .................... Tom said about Frank just can't be true.

4  The travel guide .................... I bought at the airport wasn't really very good.

5  What have you done with the documents .................... were lying on this desk?

6  Nothing .................... happens to Paul surprises me.

7  The agency .................... we used in the past didn't provide this sort of information.

8  Companies .................... workers are involved in the decision-making process are more successful.

9  You have to unlearn everything .................... you've been told before, and develop new strategies.

10  There's still something .................... worries me.

**D** **Translate these sentences.**
1  Die Chefin, die ich damals hatte, war sehr tolerant.
2  Die Leute, die wir in Indien kennen gelernt haben, waren wirkliche Experten.
3  Heute Abend treffe ich den Mann, dessen Tochter das Logo für uns entworfen hat.
4  Ich kann die Firma, die wir benutzt haben, wirklich empfehlen.
5  Das, was wir machen müssen, ist sehr einfach.

> **I spoke to** **which**
> The employee ~~to who I spoke~~ in Shanghai was German, ~~what~~ surprised me.

### Relativsätze mit Präposition

■ In den folgenden Sätzen ist das Relativpronomen nicht Subjekt des Relativsatzes. Es kann also weggelassen werden. Subjekt ist **we** bzw. **I**.

Ann is the marketing manager. We talked **to** her at the presentation.
Ann is the marketing manager **(who/that)** we talked **to** at the presentation.
*Ann ist die Marketingleiterin, mit der wir auf der Präsentation gesprochen haben.*

This is the website. I found the information **on** it .
This is the website **(which/that)** I found the information **on**.
*Dies ist die Website, auf der ich die Information gefunden habe.*

**Die Präposition (to, on) steht im Relativsatz an derselben Stelle wie vorher.**

■ Nur im formellen Englisch kann die Präposition vor dem Relativpronomen stehen. Anstelle von **who** wird dann **whom** verwendet.

The person **to whom** the offer was sent has left the company.
The forum **on which** the information was first discovered has been closed down.

### Nicht notwendige Relativsätze mit **who, which, whose**

■ Ohne den Relativsatz wären die folgenden zwei Sätze unvollständig bzw. ergäben wenig Sinn.

Employers **who pay more** have happier staff. Cars **which have an electric engine** are cleaner.

■ Die Relativsätze in den folgenden Sätzen sind dagegen entbehrlich. Sie enthalten Zusatzinformationen, die für das Verständnis nicht notwendig sind.

Angela's boss, **who by the way is younger than all of us**, speaks perfect Japanese.
*Angelas Chefin, die übrigens jünger als wir alle ist, spricht perfekt Japanisch.*
The Grand Hotel, **which is in fact very small**, was closed for repairs.
*Das Grand Hotel, das in Wirklichkeit sehr klein ist, war wegen Reparaturarbeiten geschlossen.*

■ Nicht notwendige Relativsätze werden durch **who** (Personen) oder **which** (Sachen) eingeleitet (nicht ~~that~~); **whose** ist auch möglich.

Emma, **who** (~~that~~) has two children, is my closest colleague.
The new model, **which** (~~that~~) costs €29.99, has been a complete flop.
The founders of the business, **whose** son has now taken it over, have retired to Teneriffe.

**Relativsätze dieser Art werden durch Kommas abgetrennt.**

 **which** (nicht ~~what~~) leitet entbehrliche Relativsätze ein, die sich auf einen ganzen Satz beziehen.
Tom didn't call back, **which** (~~what~~) I found strange. *Tom hat nicht zurückgerufen, was ich seltsam fand.*

### Das Wichtigste in Kürze

■ Relativsätze mit Präposition:
  ⤑ who/which/that kann man weglassen
  ⤑ die Präposition bleibt hinter dem Verb stehen (Ausnahme: in formellem Englisch)
■ Nicht notwendige Relativsätze (mit Komma):
  ⤑ who oder which (~~that~~ ist nicht möglich)
  ⤑ which (nicht ~~what~~) mit Bezug auf einen ganzen Satz

**A** **Underline the correct form.**
1 What was the name of the person  to who you complained  /  you complained to?
2 Our partners have suggested using a local design studio,  **what**  /  **which**  seems a good idea.
3 Next time I'll give the job to Martin,  **that**  /  **who**  knows more about these things than I do.
4 The photo  **at that you're looking**  /  **you're looking at**  was taken before 9/11.
5 Our taxi driver who spoke some English  /  Our taxi driver, who spoke some English,  told us about the protests.
6 The meeting will be chaired by Dr Waters,  to who you were introduced earlier  /  to whom you were introduced earlier.
7 Martin was drunk,  **what**  /  **which**  really annoyed me.

**B** **Cross out the relative pronouns which are not necessary.**
1 That's the company which we lease our cars from.
2 That's the company which supplies our cars.
3 What's the name of the Greek woman who shares the office with Jane?
4 Jane's co-worker is the Greek woman who we had lunch with last week.
5 My first job, which was very badly paid, was with a supermarket.
6 The manager of the supermarket, who was really quite nice, advised me to get some qualifications.
7 Where's the document which we were looking at earlier?
8 Documents like these, which set out everything so clearly, are really helpful.

**C** **Write questions with a relative clause.**
1 I saw you talking to a woman in the canteen. Who was it?
  What's the name of the woman ............................................................
2 You were looking for an old flyer the other day. Is this the one?
  Is this the old flyer ............................................................
3 You wrote to ten agencies, didn't you? Have you had any replies?
  Have you heard from any of the agencies ............................................................
4 The company started in someone's garage, didn't it? Is it still there?
  What has happened to the garage ............................................................
5 Karin applied for a job last month. Did she get it?
  Did Karin get the job ............................................................
6 Shall we take our visitors to a place with live music? Jack told us about one last week.
  How about taking our visitors to the restaurant with live music ............................................................

**D** **Translate the following sentences. Be careful with the commas!**
1 Frau Fuchs, die die Firma letztes Jahr verlassen hat, kannte Mr Li gut.
2 Der Kollege, auf den ich gestern gewartet habe, hatte einen Unfall.
3 Miriam hat einen Fehler gemacht, was sehr ungewöhnlich ist.
4 Mein Kollege, der aus Chile stammt, hat ein südamerikanisches Restaurant vorgeschlagen.
5 Wie ist der Name des Hotels, in dem wir letztes Jahr übernachtet haben?

> The meeting was ~~good organized~~ **well organized** and we finished it ~~surprising quick~~ **surprisingly quickly**.

## Unterschied zwischen Adjektiv und Adverb

■ Adjektive beschreiben, wie jemand/etwas ist. Sie beziehen sich auf ein Nomen oder Pronomen. Sie stehen vor einem Nomen (1) oder nach be (2).

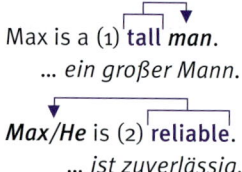

Max is a (1) **tall** *man*.
... *ein großer Mann.*

*Max/He* is (2) **reliable**.
... *ist zuverlässig.*

■ Adverbien beschreiben, wie etwas geschieht bzw. getan wird, und beziehen sich auf ein Verb (3). Sie können aber auch ein anderes Wort verstärken oder abschwächen. Dann beziehen sie sich auf ein Adjektiv (4), auf ein anderes Adverb (5) oder auf ein Partizip (6).

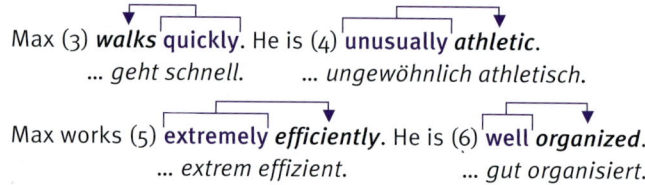

Max (3) *walks* **quickly**. He is (4) **unusually** *athletic*.
... *geht schnell.*     ... *ungewöhnlich athletisch.*

Max works (5) **extremely** *efficiently*. He is (6) **well** *organized*.
... *extrem effizient.*     ... *gut organisiert.*

## Form

■ An das Adjektiv wird meist die Endung -ly angehängt: Anna is a slow worker. She works slowly. Schreibbesonderheiten wie easy – easily, terrible – terribly, automatic – automatically (siehe Seite 126).

■ Ausnahmen sind fast (schnell) und hard (hart, schwer, heftig, kräftig). Adjektiv und Adverb sind formgleich.
I couldn't understand the Frenchman. He spoke too **fast**.                It was raining **hard**.

 Neben hard gibt es noch das Adverb hardly mit einer anderen Bedeutung (Verwechslungsgefahr!).
We work hard. *Wir arbeiten hart.* — We hardly stop. *Wir machen kaum Pausen.*

 Sonderfall good (Adjektiv) – well (Adverb): She's a good communicator. She communicates well with people.

## Verben, auf die kein Adverb folgt

Auf bestimmte Verben folgt kein Adverb, sondern ein Adjektiv. Das Bezugswort ist ein Nomen oder Pronomen, kein Verb. Es wird gesagt, wie jemand/etwas ist, nicht wie etwas getan wird.
– Verben, die einen Zustand beschreiben: seem (scheinen), become (werden), stay/remain (bleiben)
– Verben, die eine Eigenschaft ausdrücken: look (aussehen), sound (klingen, sich anhören), feel (sich fühlen, sich anfühlen), taste (schmecken), smell (riechen)
He seemed/looked excited (~~excitedly~~). *Er erschien aufgeregt. /Er sah aufgeregt aus.*

## Stellung von -ly-Adverbien

■ -ly-Adverbien, die sich auf ein Verb beziehen, stehen meist in der Satzmitte oder am Satzende.

Mit Satzmitte ist gemeint:
– vor einem allein stehenden Vollverb: The situation slowly improved.
– hinter einem Hilfsverb: The situation is slowly improving. / The situation has slowly improved.

Ein -ly-Adverb kann normalerweise nicht zwischen Verb und Objekt stehen.
I quickly finished the conversation. (~~I finished quickly the conversation.~~)

## > Das Wichtigste in Kürze

■ Ein Adjektiv sagt, wie jemand/etwas ist; ein -ly-Adverb sagt, wie etwas geschieht / getan wird
■ Kein -ly-Adverb, sondern Adjektiv u. a. nach be, seem, look, sound, feel, smell
■ Stellung: vor Vollverb, nach Hilfsverb, oder am Satzende – kein Adverb zwischen Verb und Objekt!

**A** Underline the correct form.

1  My Latvian colleague speaks English very **good** / **well**.
2  Fiona was **bad prepared** / **badly prepared** for the meeting.
3  Gwen doesn't look very **happily** / **happy**. Do you know what the problem is?
4  You always look so tired. I think you work too **hard** / **hardly**.
5  I'm afraid Mr Collins is **serious ill** / **seriously ill**.
6  When I saw Ray and Matilda in the room, I **quietly closed the door** / **closed quietly the door** again.
7  Roland was **bad hurt** / **badly hurt** in the car accident.
8  I looked **quick** / **quickly** at my watch.
9  Could we have a moment to **read quickly the document** / **quickly read the document**, please?
10  I don't know Mr Li **particular good** / **particularly well**. I've only met him once.

**B** Rewrite these sentences using an adverb instead of an adjective.

1  David is an extremely **slow** eater. David eats ...........................................................

2  They are **fast** workers. They work ...........................................................

3  We have **regular** meetings. We meet ...........................................................

4  His death was completely **unexpected**. He died ...........................................................

5  Your German is really **good**. You speak German ...........................................................

**C** Complete these conversations with adjectives or adverbs.

1  A: I'm ..................... (extreme/extremely) tired. I've been so ..................... (busy/busily).
   B: Be ................... (careful/carefully) that you don't work too ................. (hard/hardly).
   A: I won't. I've been sleeping ............. (bad/badly) – that's the .............. (real/really) problem.
2  A: Hello, Sandra! Did you have a ................ (good/well) trip? What was your hotel like?
   B: I ................ (hard/hardly) ever sleep ................ (good/well) on a business trip, but it was
   ................... (unusual/unusually) ................... (quiet/quietly).
3  A: What's the matter with Marek? He seems so ................... (anxious/anxiously).
   B: He's been ................... (terrible/terribly) worried about losing his job since the management
   changed ..................... (sudden/suddenly) last month.
   A: His job is quite ................... (good/well) paid, isn't it? So they might try to cut it. They're always
   trying to do things as ................... (cheap/cheaply) as possible.
4  A: I've just heard that we've lost the contract. You must be ............... (bitter/bitterly) disappointed.
   B: Yes, I'm ................... (thorough/thoroughly) fed up. I think Martin's department let me down.
5  A: This office is so ................... (noisy/noisily), I can't concentrate on my work ...................
   (proper/properly).
   B: Well, if you ask the ................. boss (nice/nicely), perhaps he'll do something about it.

**D** Complete the sentences by ticking the correct position for the adverbs in brackets.

1  Gina **A** [ ] learned **B** [ ] the new procedure. **(quickly)**
2  We completed **A** [ ] the negotiations **B** [ ]. **(successfully)**
3  Sales **A** [ ] are **B** [ ] recovering. **(gradually)**
4  I can **A** [ ] find out **B** [ ] the address on the internet. **(easily)**
5  I wish Mr Asai would explain **A** [ ] things **B** [ ]. **(occasionally)**
6  In the recesssion companies dropped **A** [ ] their prices **B** [ ]. **(dramatically)**

**E** Translate the following sentences.

1  John fühlte sich fürchterlich. Er war fürchterlich müde.
2  Ich fing langsam an zu verstehen, warum Martina skeptisch blieb.
3  Wir fanden überraschend leicht einen Parkplatz.
4  Sie sehen sehr enttäuscht aus. Was ist passiert?

| | | New mail | |
|---|---|---|---|
| To: | | | |

*much better than*                                             *as*
Sales are ~~much more better as~~ last year. It's the same situation ~~like~~ after the last recession.

**Steigerungsformen von Adjektiven**
■ Durch Anhängen von -er/-est werden gesteigert:
  – einsilbige Adjektive (Schreibbesonderheiten siehe Seite 126): high – higher – highest
  – zweisilbige Adjektive auf -y (angry, dirty, easy, funny, happy, lovely, lucky usw.)
    Dabei wird y zu i: easy – easier – easiest.

■ Durch Voranstellen von more/most werden gesteigert:
  – mehrsilbige Adjektive (außer zweisilbige auf -y): careful – more careful – most careful

■ Ausnahmen und Sonderformen
  good – better – best  *gut – besser – beste(r/s)*
  bad – worse – worst  *schlecht – schlechter – schlechteste(r/s)*
  far – farther/further – farthest/furthest  *weit – weiter – weiteste(r/s)*

Einige Adjektive kann man sowohl mit -er/-est als auch mit more/most steigern: clear, fair, safe, true, busy, friendly, healthy, likely, lively, wealthy, clever, common, narrow, pleasant, quiet, simple.

**Vergleiche**
■ Setzt man zwei Personen/Dinge gleich, wird der Vergleichssatz mit as gebildet.
  I'm as old as Phil. *Ich bin (genau) so alt wie Phil.*
  I'm not as qualified as Ann. *Ich bin nicht so qualifiziert wie Ann.*

**!** Auch nach the same steht as: My pay is the same as (~~like~~) it was last year.

■ Nach Adjektiven in der ersten Steigerungsstufe wird nicht as, sondern than gebraucht.
  Dave is older than (~~as~~) his boss. *Dave ist älter als seine Chefin.*
  The new model is more expensive than (~~as~~) the previous one. *… teurer als das vorherige.*
  It was colder than (~~as~~) I had expected. *Es war kälter, als ich erwartet hatte.*

■ Mit less und (the) least drückt man das Gegenteil von more und (the) most aus.
  Jack's promotion was less surprising than Gina's. *Jacks Beförderung war weniger überraschend als Ginas.*
  Ed's was the least interesting presentation. *… die am wenigsten interessante Präsentation.*

■ Nach as bzw. than stehen allein stehende Personalpronomen in der Objektform.
  Don isn't as patient as me. I'm more patient than him. *… nicht so geduldig wie ich. … geduldiger als er.*

**next und nearest, newest und latest**
■ next bezeichnet das (zeitlich oder räumlich) Nächstfolgende, nearest das Nächstgelegene.
  Take the next street on the right. *Nehmen Sie die nächste Straße rechts.*
  The nearest hotel is two miles from the conference centre. *Das nächste/nächstgelegene Hotel …*

**!** newest ist das Gegenteil von oldest; latest bezeichnet das Neuste/Aktuellste/ bisher Letzte.
This office block is the newest in this part of town. *Dieses Bürohaus ist das neuste in diesem Stadtteil.*
Our latest model has of course all the latest technology. *Unser neustes Modell … die (aller)neuste Technik.*

**Das Wichtigste in Kürze**
■ Steigerung: Kurze Adjektive: -er/-est; längere Adjektive: more/most
■ Vergleiche: Bei Gleichsetzung: as; in der ersten Steigerungsstufe: than

**A** Underline the correct form.

1 Mr Li is **easier** / **easyer** to understand than Mr Asai.
2 My office is almost **as** / **so** big as Karen's.
3 Greg's Spanish is **much better** / **much more better** than mine.
4 Flying is **cheaper** / **more cheap** than going by train.
5 Taiwan is our **importantest** / **most important** overseas market.
6 I work longer hours **as** / **than** most of my colleagues.
7 I'm taking my holidays at the same time **as** / **like** you.
8 Rachel and I are in the same department, but I have more experience than **her** / **she**.
9 Which is the **nearest** / **next** underground station to the hotel?

**B** Make comparisons and add **as** or **than** if necessary.

1 Is it much . . . . . . . . . . . . . . . . . . . . . . (hard) to find a job today . . . . . . . . . . . . . . . . . . . . . . it was ten years ago?

2 Diesel costs the same . . . . . . . . . . . . . . . . . . . . . . . petrol. In most countries petrol is

. . . . . . . . . . . . . . . . . . . . . . (expensive) . . . . . . . . . . . . . . . . . . . . . . diesel.

3 It's much . . . . . . . . . . . . . . . . . . . . . . (difficult) to find an apartment . . . . . . . . . . . . . . . . . . . . . . I expected.

4 The Bulgarian company has quoted the . . . . . . . . . . . . . . . . . . . . . . (low) price, but I'm not sure that it's

really the . . . . . . . . . . . . . . . . . . . . . . (good) offer.

5 The recession is . . . . . . . . . . . . . . . . . . . . . . (serious) . . . . . . . . . . . . . . . . . . . . . . economists first thought.

6 What's the . . . . . . . . . . . . . . . . . . . . . . (bad) thing that has ever happened to you?

7 All our options are risky. The question is: Which is the . . . . . . . . . . . . . . . . . . . . . . (less risky)?

**C** Complete the sentences using comparatives and superlatives.

1 This restaurant is too expensive. Can we go to a . . . . . . . . . . . . . . . . . . . one?

2 This conference room is too small. We need a . . . . . . . . . . . . . . . . . . . one.

3 The 8 o'clock flight won't get us to Lyon before 12. We need to get the . . . . . . . . . . . . . . . . . . . one at 6.30.

4 I don't think the XMK 1 is on the market any more. The . . . . . . . . . . . . . . . . . . . model is the XMK 2.

5 Where can I plug my projector in? Where's the . . . . . . . . . . . . . . . . . . . electrical socket?

**D** Translate the following sentences.

1 Der Flug dauert viel länger als ich dachte.
2 Du hast den gleichen Computer wie ich.
3 Dieses Jahr ist unser Hotel weiter weg von der Messe als letztes Jahr.
4 Der Katalog ist dünner als letztes Jahr.
5 Im Mai hatten wir die schlechtesten Verkäufe seit 2008.
6 Wer hat die neueste Preisliste?
7 Wo ist der nächste Taxistand?
8 Mark ist qualifizierter als ich, aber mein Gehalt ist höher als seins.
9 Die lustigste Episode passierte mir in Hongkong.
10 Ist Lösung A oder Lösung B weniger aufwändig (expensive)?

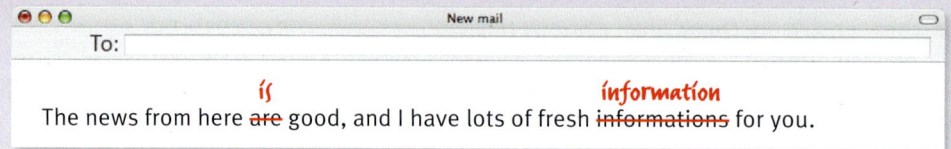

*is* *information*
The news from here ~~are~~ good, and I have lots of fresh ~~informations~~ for you.

### Zählbare Nomen – nichtzählbare Nomen

- Viele Nomen sind zählbar, z. B. **computer**: a/one computer, two computers, three computers.
  Manche Nomen sind nicht zählbar, z. B. **money**: ~~a/one money, two moneys~~, …
  Nichtzählbare Nomen haben **keine** Mehrzahlform und man kann **kein** a/an davor setzen.

Letzteres gilt auch, wenn ein Adjektiv vor dem Nomen steht.
What (~~What a~~) **fantastic weather**! *Was für ein tolles Wetter!*
You speak **excellent** (~~an excellent~~) German. *Sie sprechen ein ausgezeichnetes Deutsch.*
**terrible traffic** *ein furchtbarer Verkehr*, **interesting feedback** *ein interessantes Feedback*
**absolute chaos** *ein absolutes Chaos*, **lots of luck/stress** *ein großes Glück / ein großer Stress*

### Zählbar im Deutschen – nichtzählbar im Englischen

Bestimmte Nomen, die im Deutschen zählbar sind, sind es im Englischen nicht.
That **is** useful **information**. (~~Those are useful informations~~.) *Das sind nützliche Informationen.*
Ellen's **advice is** always good. (~~Ellen's advices are always good~~.) *Ellens Ratschläge sind immer gut.*
How**'s business**? *Wie laufen die Geschäfte?*

| | |
|---|---|
| **information** *Information(en)* | **homework** *Hausaufgabe(n)* |
| **news** *Nachricht(en)* | **damage** *Schaden, Schäden* |
| **advice** *Rat, Ratschläge* | **knowledge** *Wissen, Kenntnis(se)* |
| **help** *Hilfe(n)* | **progress** *Fortschritt(e)* |
| **equipment** *Gerät(e), Ausrüstung(sgegenstand)* | **evidence** *Beweis(e)* |
| **machinery** *Maschinen* | **proof** *Beweis(e)* |
| **business** *Geschäft(e)* | **hair** *Haar(e)* |
| **work** *Arbeit(en)* | **furniture** *Möbel* |

- Vor einem nichtzählbaren Nomen kann **some, any, a lot of, much** stehen (aber **nicht** ~~many~~).
  She gave me **some** important **advice**. *Sie gab mir wichtige Ratschläge.*
  The trainer didn't give us **any homework**. *Die Ausbilderin gab uns keine Hausaufgaben.*
  We have **a lot of information** (~~many informations~~) now. *Wir haben jetzt viele Informationen.*
  How **much proof** is there? (~~How many proofs are there?~~) *Wie viele Beweise gibt es?*

- Nichtzählbare Nomen kann man häufig mit **a bit/piece of** zählbar machen.
  Margaret has **a bit of news** for you. *Margaret hat eine Neuigkeit für dich.*
  **Two bits of information** are still missing. *Zwei Informationen fehlen noch.*
  I'll give you **a piece of advice**. *Ich gebe Ihnen einen Rat.*

- Die zählbare Entsprechung von deutsch „Arbeit" heißt **job** oder **task**.
  Michaela has found **a** new **job** at last. *… eine neue Arbeit …*
  Writing minutes is **a job/task** I hate. *Protokoll schreiben ist eine Arbeit, die ich hasse.*

### Das Wichtigste in Kürze

- Nichtzählbare Nomen: **keine** Mehrzahlform, **keine** Verwendung von ~~a/an~~ oder ~~many~~
- Nichtzählbar im Englischen u. a.: **advice, help, information, work, damage, progress**

**A** **Underline the correct form.**
1 This information is / These informations are very interesting.
2 Max gave me a good advice / some good advice.
3 What knowledge / knowledges and skills would someone need to do your job?
4 How many damages / much damage did the fire cause?
5 What a wonderful news! / What wonderful news!
6 There are certain jobs / works in this department that we really have to finish by Friday evening.
7 These three things are the only specialist equipment / equipments I need in my job.
8 Isabella's new leather furniture has / furnitures have arrived.

**B** **Correct any plural forms which are not possible.**

1 Although Arthur always does all his assignments, he doesn't seem to make a lot of progresses.

2 A personal coach can give you a lot of useful advices. Mine gave me a lot of informations about online management training courses.

3 The amount of money a big organization spends on furnitures and office equipments is enormous.

4 I have a lot of works at the moment. My boss always gives me more jobs to do than my colleagues.

5 The closed circuit TV recordings provided the police with some helps, and two people have been identified, but the police still don't have any proofs that they carried out the break-in.

**C** **Complete the following dialogues by underlining the correct forms.**

1 A: I have such a lot of work/works at the moment.
   B: Do you think you will finish it/them before your holiday?

2 A: Your hair/hairs looks/look nice.
   B: Thanks. I had it/them cut yesterday.

3 A: What equipment/equipments should our technicians bring with them?
   B: I'll send you an email with precise information/informations.

4 A: Do you want anything else from the buffet? Another bread / Another piece of bread? More fruit?
   B: No, thanks. Let's finish breakfast and walk to their offices. It's such a lovely / such lovely weather.

5 A: Stella has just been offered that job in Florence. I'm sure it's because she speaks such good / such a good Italian.
   B: And I hear that you're going to the London office for two months. So that's two good news / two pieces of good news in one day.

**D** **Translate the following sentences.**
1 Haben sie genügend Beweise, dass Gelder auf geheimen Konten „versteckt" wurden?
2 Dieses Jahr haben Sie viele Fortschritte gemacht.
3 Tom Hughes ist leicht zu erkennen. Seine Haare sind rot und sehr lang.
4 Magda spricht gut Französisch und ihre Spanischkenntnisse sind nicht schlecht.

> dollars them
> Is this figure 200 ~~dollar~~ or 300? I can't see without my glasses, and I don't know where I've put ~~it~~.

### Nomen, die es nur in der Mehrzahl gibt

„Paarwörter" bezeichnen Dinge, die aus zwei gleichen Teilen bestehen. Diese gibt es im Englischen nur in der Mehrzahl.

Where **are** my **glasses**? **They were** here a moment ago. *Wo ist meine Brille? Sie war eben noch da.*
**These** red **jeans are** something I couldn't wear in the office. *Diese rote Jeans ist etwas …*
**These scissors are** very sharp. *Diese Schere ist sehr scharf.*

Als Ersatz für eine Einzahlform kann man **a pair of** verwenden.
I need **a** good **pair of trousers** / **a pair of sunglasses**. *Ich brauche eine gute Hose / eine Sonnenbrille.*

| | | | |
|---|---|---|---|
| **glasses** *Brille(n)* | **binoculars** *Fernglas/-gläser* | **jeans** *Jeans* | **shorts** *Shorts* |
| **scissors** *Schere(n)* | **headphones** *Kopfhörer* | **trousers** *Hose(n)* | **pyjamas** *Pyjama(s)* |

Auch **police** *(Polizei)*, **people** *(Leute/Menschen)*, **goods** *(Ware/n)*, **premises** *(Geschäftsräume)*, **stairs** *(Treppe/n)*, **clothes** *(Kleidung)*, **thanks** *(Dank)*, **surroundings** *(Umgebung)*, **outskirts** *(Stadtrand)* gibt es nur in der Mehrzahl.

The **police are** (~~is~~) here. **They are** (~~It is~~) looking everywhere. *Die Polizei ist da. Sie sucht überall.*
Cotton **clothes are** better in warmer weather. *Baumwollkleidung ist besser bei wärmerem Wetter.*

Beachten Sie: **the United States / the US / the USA** stehen mit einem Verb in der Einzahl.
**The United States is** (~~are~~) a rich country. *Die Vereinigten Staaten sind ein reiches Land.*

### Mengenangaben mit Zahlen, Maßeinheiten, Währungen

Maßeinheiten und Währungen haben – wie fast alle anderen Nomen – in der Mehrzahl ein **-s**.
ten kilometre**s** *zehn Kilometer*    six litre**s** *sechs Liter*    two pound**s**/dollar**s** *zwei Pfund/Dollar*

Ein Verb folgt jedoch in der Einzahl, wenn ein Betrag, eine Menge oder Entfernung gemeint ist.
**1000 dollars is** (~~are~~) a lot of money. **Three kilometres isn't** (~~aren't~~) far. **70 years is** (~~are~~) a long time.

Wenn ein Nomen mit Zahl + Bindestrich vor einem anderen Nomen steht und diese Wendung die Funktion eines Adjektivs hat, entfällt das Mehrzahl-**s**.
an **18-hour day** *ein 18-Stundentag*  a **four-star hotel** *ein Vier-Sterne-Hotel*

Das Zahlwort **million** steht (wie **hundred** und **thousand**) nach einem anderen Zahlwort ohne **-s**.
**6 million** (~~millions~~) people *6 Millionen Menschen*    **ten million** (~~millions~~)    **two hundred** thousand

> ### Das Wichtigste in Kürze
> - Immer Mehrzahl: „Paarwörter"
> - Immer Mehrzahl: police, goods, stairs, thanks, …
> - Maßeinheiten, Währungen mit -s: ten metres, six dollars
> - Mengen und Beträge mit Verb in der Einzahl: Two hours is a long time.
> - „Bindestrich-Adjektive" ohne -s: a four-star hotel

**A** **Underline the correct form.**

1  We stayed in  **a five-star hotel  /  a five-stars hotel**.
2  **A designer sunglasses is  /  A pair of designer sunglasses is**  much cheaper in Eastern Europe.
3  We have  **a three-year-old  /  a three-years-old**  daughter.
4  The firm invested  **ten million  /  ten millions**  in the project.
5  **Has  /  Have**  the police given any more information?
6  The goods  **hasn't  /  haven't**  reached the factory yet.
7  Five thousand euros  **doesn't sound  /  don't sound**  a high price to pay.
8  **Is  /  Are**  the United States still the market leader?

**B** **Singular or plural? Fill in the correct form of the verb.**

1  I need to change into something cooler, but my shorts ................... still in my suitcase.

2  Two kilometres ................... too far to walk with a suitcase. Let's take a taxi.

3  Your glasses ................... cool, really great.

4  The police ................... just come.

5  Those stairs ................... dangerous. We really must get someone to repair them.

6  200 dollars ................... a lot of money for a courier service.

7  When you're nervous, twenty-five minutes ................... a long time to wait.

8  The new premises ................... just been opened.

**C** **Make complete questions.**

1  Why ................... clothes manufactured in Asia cheaper?

2  How much ................... your new sunglasses?

3  I've got my iPod™, but where ................... my headphones?

4  What do you think – ................... nine hundred dollars too high a price?

5  ................... six litres per 100 kilometres a lot for this size of car?

6  Which drawer ................... the scissors in?

7  This place we are going to – what ................... the location like? ................... the surroundings nice?

**D** **Translate the following sentences.**

1  Berlin ist 1200 Kilometer von hier.
2  Die Vereinigten Staaten sind unser bester Kunde.
3  Die richtige Kleidung ist sehr wichtig für ein Vorstellungsgespräch.
4  Ist dieses Fernglas aus Japan?
5  Ich habe eine 60-Stundenwoche.
6  Mehr als drei Millionen Menschen sind arbeitslos.
7  Das Land hat 20 Millionen Einwohner.
8  Der Stadtrand ist sehr grün.

# 40 The definite article *the*
## Der bestimmte Artikel *the*

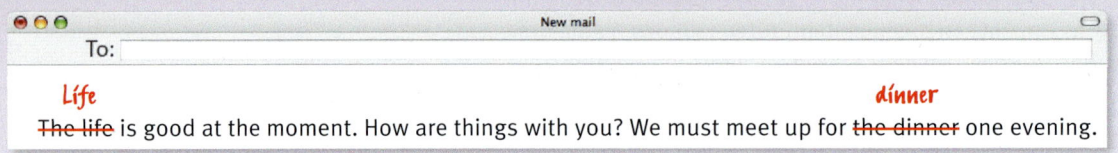

New mail

To:

*Life*                                                                                    *dinner*

~~The life~~ is good at the moment. How are things with you? We must meet up for ~~the dinner~~ one evening.

## Das Weglassen von *the* bei abstrakten Nomen

In allgemeinen Aussagen stehen abstrakte und Mehrzahlnomen ohne *the*.

(~~The~~) **Life** is good. *Das Leben …*                    (~~The~~) **Nature** can tell us a lot. *Die Natur …*
We spend a lot on (~~the~~) **security**. *… die Sicherheit …*    (~~The~~) **People** love (~~the~~) **money**. *Die Menschen lieben*
(~~The~~) **History** is full of wars. *Die Geschichte …*                                            *das Geld.*

Dies gilt auch, wenn vor dem Nomen ein Adjektiv oder danach eine Fügung mit Präposition steht.
What do you know about (~~the~~) **Chinese history**?        (~~The~~) **Life in Soviet times** was hard.

Wenn jedoch die Präposition *of* heißt, oder ein Relativsatz folgt, kann man *the* **nicht** weglassen.
What do you know about **the life of Bill Gates**?        **The life** (that) **I'd like to live** is impossible.

## Das Weglassen von *the* bei school, prison, church usw.

■ Wenn man an den Zweck dieser Einrichtungen denkt (**nicht** an das Gebäude/Bauwerk) und von deren
Nutzern spricht (Schülern/Gefangenen/Kirchgängern), entfällt *the*.
Did you like **school**? *die Schule*                    **Aber:** Turn left at **the school**.
A terrorist escaped from **prison**. *aus dem Gefängnis*    **Aber:** The police are at **the prison** now.
Not many people go to **church**. *in die Kirche*        **Aber:** **The church** was built in 1560.

■ Im britischen Englisch stehen **university** und **hospital** ohne, im amerikanischen Englisch mit *the*.
What did you study (BE) **at university** / (AE) **at the university**?  **Aber:** **The university** is 200 years old.
Ed will be (BE) **in hospital** / (AE) **in the hospital** for a week.    **Aber:** Where is **the** nearest **hospital**?

 *the* entfällt, wenn die Universität / das Krankenhaus mit Eigennamen genannt wird.
**Harvard University** is the oldest in the USA.        The man was taken to **Bethesda Hospital**.

■ *the* entfällt auch bei **in/to bed** (in Verbindung mit Schlafen), **home** und **work**.
When did he go **to bed** last night? Is he still **in bed**?        What time do you leave **home/work**?

## Das Weglassen von *the* bei Eigennamen, nicht näher bestimmten Mahlzeiten, Verkehrsmitteln

■ Im Gegensatz zum deutschen Sprachgebrauch entfällt der Artikel vor:
  – Eigennamen der meisten Straßen, Plätze, Brücken und Parks und vieler Gebäude:
    We met in (~~in the~~) **Park Street** / at (~~at the~~) **Frankfurt Airport** / near (~~near the~~) **Victoria Station**.
  – Eigennamen von Wochentagen und Monaten: We met **on Monday** / **in May**.
  – Eigennamen von Seen und Bergen (**nicht** Gebirgen): **Lake Constance** / **Mount Everest** is big.
  – Eigennamen, denen ein Adjektiv vorausgeht: **old Don**, **clever Google**, **modern America**
  – Mahlzeiten: When's **lunch**? Let's talk **after lunch**. (Aber: **The lunch** I had yesterday was …)
  – by + Verkehrsmittel: I came **by car/bus/train/plane**. (Aber: take **the bus/train**)

## > Das Wichtigste in Kürze
■ *the* entfällt:
  – vor abstrakten Nomen (außer wenn *of* oder ein Relativsatz folgt)
  – oft vor Namen von Einrichtungen wie **school**, **church**
  – vor Eigennamen und Mahlzeiten

**A** **Underline the correct form.**
1 After lunch / the lunch we went for a walk.
2 Children in Asia work hard in school / in the school.
3 Crime / The crime has increased in recent years.
4 I usually get to the work / to work at 8 o'clock.
5 It's been a long day. I need to get to bed / to the bed.
6 Life / The life is not easy.
7 The Tower Bridge / Tower Bridge has been closed for repairs.

**B** **Cross out any articles which are incorrect.**

1 The travel business is changing. The old people are a big market these days.

2 I didn't go to the work yesterday. I stayed in the bed because I didn't feel well.

3 It's not only the car industry that has been hit by this recession. The industry as a whole has been affected.

4 I studied International Business at the Cressex University. The university is well known for its business courses.

5 All the people in this company are in favour of the nuclear energy. We are in the energy industry.

6 The music is very important to me. I love the classical music.

**C** **Fill in the where necessary.**

1 Last year we spent our holiday in ..... Turkey. Our hotel was great – we had ..... breakfast there and went to a restaurant for ..... dinner.

2 My son wants to go to ..... university in ..... United States. Before he starts his course, he hopes to go to ..... Rocky Mountains.

3 A lot of ..... people don't buy a printed newspaper any more.

4 When I go to Brussels on ..... business, I usually go by ..... train. I'm usually home for ..... supper.

5 ..... flight landed at ..... Gatwick Airport, then we took ..... train to London.

6 ..... life in ..... modern India is so different from ..... life in ..... traditional India.

**D** **Translate the following sentences.**
1 Ist der Mont Blanc in der Schweiz?
2 Die britische Küche (cuisine) ist besser, als die Leute meinen.
3 Ein „normaler" Beruf ist sicherer. Man kann mit der Kunst nie das große Geld verdienen.
4 Ich nehme nie den Bus – ich fahre immer mit dem Auto zur Arbeit.
5 Man muss vorsichtig sein. Man kann leicht im Gefängnis landen.
6 Warum wollen die Leute immer mehr Geld?
7 Der kluge Max hat immer einen Plan B.
8 Auf Geschäftsreisen habe ich nie Zeit. Ich habe die großen Sehenswürdigkeiten nie gesehen – den Roten Platz in Moskau, die Tower Bridge in London, die Fifth Avenue in New York.
9 Es lohnt sich immer, etwas über die Geschichte eines Landes zu wissen.

# 41 The indefinite article *a/an*
## Der unbestimmte Artikel *a/an*

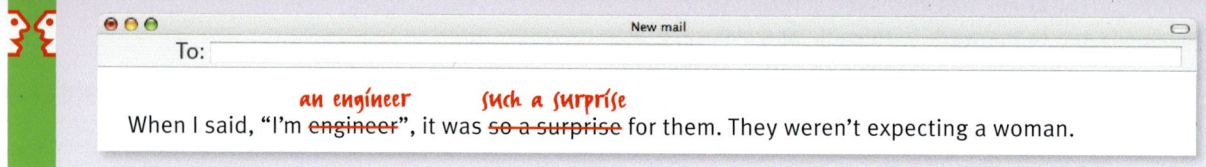

When I said, "I'm ~~engineer~~ **an engineer**", it was ~~so a surprise~~ **such a surprise** for them. They weren't expecting a woman.

**!** **Englisch: unbestimmter Artikel – Deutsch: kein Artikel**

Im Englischen steht manchmal der unbestimmte Artikel, wo im Deutschen kein Artikel nötig ist.

| | |
|---|---|
| – Berufsangaben | Anja is **a technician**. Max is **a marketing person**. |
| – Nationalitätsangaben | Ed is **an Englishman**. (= Ed is English.) |
| – Angaben zu politischer/<br>religiöser Überzeugung | Sarah is **a social democrat**.<br>Peter is **a Buddhist**. |
| – Angaben zu Genuss-<br>und Sportgewohnheiten | Regina is **a vegetarian** and **a non-smoker**.<br>Angela is **a jogger** and **a tennis player**. |
| – vor **member, expert, millionaire,**<br>**optimist** und **pessimist** | Is she **a member** / **an expert** / **a millionaire**?<br>Roland is always **an optimist** / **a pessimist**. |
| – vor **headache** und **cold** | I have **a headache** / **a cold**. |
| – nach **as** | **As a** lawyer I deal with contracts all the time. |

**!** **a/an in der Bedeutung „pro"**

**Nicht** der bestimmte Artikel, sondern der unbestimmte Artikel wird in der Bedeutung „pro" vor Zeit-, Maß- und Mengenangaben gebraucht.

We meet **twice a week**. ... *zwei Mal die Woche.*
People walk about **four miles an hour**. ... *vier Meilen in der Stunde.*
They cost **two euros a kilo**. ... *zwei Euro das Kilo.*

**!** **half, such, quite + a/an**

**a/an** steht hinter **half** und **such**, **nicht** davor.
I'll see you in **half an hour**. ... *in einer halben Stunde.*
It was **such a nice day**. ... *so ein schöner Tag.*

Vor einem (Adjektiv + ) Nomen kann **so** **nicht** stehen.
He's **such** (~~so~~) **an idiot**.     He's **such** (~~so~~) **a stupid man**.

■ **a/an** steht meist hinter **quite**. In Verbindung mit einem Adjektiv + Nomen kann es davor stehen.
   We got **quite a shock** (~~a quite shock~~). ... *einen ziemlichen Schock.*
   It was **quite a long journey** / **a quite long journey**. ... *eine ziemlich lange Reise.*

**!** **Kein a/an mit nichtzählbaren Nomen**

Vor einem nichtzählbaren Nomen kann **a/an** **nicht** stehen (siehe Unit 38).
What (~~What a~~) wonderful **weather**! *Was für ein wunderbares Wetter!*

**>** **Das Wichtigste in Kürze**

■ **a/an** nach **as** und bei Angaben zu Beruf, Überzeugung, Gewohnheiten
■ **a/an** vor **member, expert, millionaire** usw.
■ **a/an** (**nicht** ~~the~~) in der Bedeutung „pro"
■ **a/an** hinter **half, such** – **nicht** davor
■ Kein ~~a/an~~ vor nichtzählbaren Nomen

**A** **Underline the correct form.**

1 My wife is **a doctor** / **doctor**.
2 I go to an English class **once a week** / **once the week**.
3 Ronald is **so an idiot** / **such an idiot**!
4 Let's meet in **a half hour** / **half an hour**.
5 My Chinese boss is **a chain smoker** / **chain smoker**.
6 Are you **a member** / **member** of any political organization?
7 **As a sign** / **As sign** of our good will we will bear the transport costs.

**B** **Make sentences with these items. There is always one item that you don't need.**

1 a / day. / It's / lovely / so / such

.................................................................................................................

2 a / an / half / hour. / going to / It's / take us

.................................................................................................................

3 a / a big conference / have / in the / We / twice / year.

.................................................................................................................

4 a / an / half / have / litre of red wine, please. / We'll

.................................................................................................................

5 a / got / shock. / so / such / We all

.................................................................................................................

6 about / an / hour. / 100 kilometres / the / The taxi driver / was going

.................................................................................................................

**C** **Add an indefinite article where necessary.**

1 One of my colleagues is ...... football fanatic, the other is ...... anarchist!

2 I have ...... terrible headache. – Shall I get you ...... aspirin?

3 As ...... trainee you work in several different departments.

4 I've never seen such ...... terrible traffic. I've never had ...... journey like this.

5 I'm afraid I'm not much of ...... expert on wine. Shall we have ...... bottle of Portuguese red?

6 We had ...... wonderful weather all the time we were there.

7 In my job I'm usually away from the office travelling about ten days ...... month.

8 My daughter is ...... student. She wants to become ...... designer.

**D** **Translate the following sentences.**

1 Sandras Büro hat so eine fantastische Aussicht.
2 Was für eine gute Idee!
3 Ich arbeite etwa 60 Stunden in der Woche.
4 Wir bekamen so einen Schock, als sie uns sagten, dass die Fabrik schließen würde.
5 Es war ein Vergnügen, mit Ihnen zu arbeiten.
6 Ich glaube, ich bekomme eine Erkältung. Ich habe Kopfschmerzen.
7 Mein Kollege ist Nichtraucher.
8 Sind Sie Arzt? Wir brauchen Hilfe.
9 Vier von Tinas alten Kolleginnen wurden als Überraschung eingeladen.

> meet
> If you can afford the time, maybe we could ~~meet us~~ for a game of golf.

## Formen

| | | | | |
|---|---|---|---|---|
| Einzahl: | -self | **myself** | **yourself** | **himself, herself, itself** |
| | | *mir/mich selbst* | *dir/dich/[Sie] sich selbst* | *sich selbst* |
| Mehrzahl: | -selves | **ourselves** | **yourselves** | **themselves** |
| | | *uns selbst* | *euch/[Sie] sich selbst* | *sich selbst* |

## Gebrauch im Rückbezug auf das Subjekt

■ Im Englischen verwendet man im Rückbezug auf das Subjekt keine Personalpronomen.

**We** got **ourselves** (~~us~~) ready. *Wir machten uns bereit.*
**I** taught **myself** (~~me~~) Thai. *Ich habe mir selbst Thailändisch beigebracht.*
**Rosalind** can take care of **herself**. *Rosalind kann auf sich selbst aufpassen.*
**Help yourselves**, and **enjoy yourselves**! *Bedienen Sie sich und haben Sie viel Spaß!*

Ausnahme: nach Präpositionen des Ortes (**in front of**, **behind**, **with** usw.)
Tom heard a noise **behind him** (~~himself~~). *... hinter sich.*    He had a lot of money **with him**. *... bei sich.*

**!** **each other** (oder **one another**) entspricht „uns/euch/sich" im Sinne von „uns/euch/sich gegenseitig".
**We** help **each other** (~~us~~) when one of us has a problem. *Wir helfen uns gegenseitig ...*
After 20 years of working together **they** know **each other** (~~them~~) very well. *... kennen sie sich sehr gut.*

**!** Deutsche Reflexivverben entsprechen nicht immer Reflexivverben im Englischen.
We can't **afford** that. *Wir können uns das nicht leisten.*
When will he **decide**? *Wann entscheidet er sich?*

| | | |
|---|---|---|
| **afford** *sich leisten* | **feel** *sich fühlen* | **rely on** *sich verlassen auf* |
| **apologize** *sich entschuldigen* | **hurry** *sich beeilen* | **remember** *sich erinnern* |
| **argue** *sich streiten* | **imagine** *sich vorstellen* | **rest** *sich ausruhen* |
| **be interested in** *sich interessieren für* | **lie down** *sich hinlegen* | **sit down** *sich setzen* |
| **change** *sich umziehen; sich verändern* | **meet** *sich treffen* | **wonder** *sich fragen* |
| **complain** *sich beschweren* | **relax** *sich ausruhen /* | **worry** *sich Sorgen machen* |
| **concentrate** *sich konzentrieren* | *sich entspannen* | |

## Gebrauch zur Hervorhebung = deutsch „selbst/selber"

■ Reflexivpronomen dienen auch der Hervorhebung. Sie entsprechen dann „selbst/selber".

**We** designed the logo **ourselves**. *Wir haben das Logo selbst entworfen.*
**Roland** has done everything **himself**. *Roland hat alles selber gemacht.*

> ## Das Wichtigste in Kürze
>
> ■ Einzahl: **-self** — Mehrzahl: **-selves**
> ■ „uns/euch/sich gegenseitig" = **each other**
> ■ Wichtige deutsche Reflexivverben sind keine Reflexivverben im Englischen:
> *sich fühlen* (**feel**), *sich konzentrieren* (**concentrate**), *sich vorstellen* (**imagine**), *sich treffen* (**meet**),
> *sich Sorgen machen* (**worry**) usw.

**A** Underline the correct form.

1 Be careful, or you'll **hurt you** / **hurt yourself**.
2 It's difficult to **concentrate** / **concentrate yourself** with all this noise.
3 I'm sorry, but I don't have any time to help you. You'll have to get everything ready **self** / **yourself**.
4 When are we **meeting** / **meeting us**?
5 I'm afraid I haven't got enough cash on **me** / **myself**. Could you lend me some?
6 I **remember** / **remember me** how I met Elena in Moscow once.
7 How long have we known **each other** / **us** now?
8 My company didn't pay. I paid for **me** / **myself**.
9 Please **help you** / **help yourselves** to coffee and water.

**B** Complete these sentences with the translation of the verbs in brackets.

1 (sich fühlen) How ............................ today? Did you have a better night?

2 (sich fragen) I ............................ how much all this will cost.

3 (sich vorstellen) I can't ............................ why anyone would want to buy one of these things.

4 (sich erzählen) Jackie and I have no secrets. We ............................ everything.

5 (sich verletzen) Are you all right? Have you ............................?

6 (sich sehen) I can't ............................ in this job for much longer. I need a change.

7 (sich konzentrieren) It was hot and everyone was tired. Nobody could ............................

properly.

**C** If necessary, add the correct reflexive pronouns or **each other**.

1 Don, please don't blame ................... for what happened. It was my fault as much as it was yours.

2 At the training seminar we got to know ................... well.

3 My husband is English so we speak to ................... in English most of the time.

4 What time are you and Mr Li meeting ...................?

5 Juliana doesn't have a business partner, she does everything ...................

6 We believe in teamwork, so people who only think about ................... are not welcome.

7 Sue and her colleague are very different personalities, but they really seem to like ...................

8 Please relax ................... and make ................... at home. Help ................... if you

would like something to drink.

9 I can't afford ................... to go on holiday this year.

10 Max and I haven't seen ................... since the conference in Milan two years ago.

11 Everything is going to be all right. Please don't worry ...................

**D** Translate the following sentences.

1 Ich frage mich, ob Sandra ihre Kollegen informiert hat.
2 Der Raum war nicht fertig. Wir haben uns bei den Organisatoren beschwert.
3 Wir treffen uns um acht, aber ich kann mich nicht erinnern, wo.
4 Ich ziehe es vor, wichtige Texte selbst zu schreiben.
5 Wir haben zwei Stunden Zeit vor der Sitzung. Ich will mich hinlegen und ein bisschen ausruhen.
6 Herr Beck und Herr Lima stritten sich zwei Stunden lang.
7 Kann ich mich auf ihn verlassen?
8 Wofür interessieren Sie sich am meisten?

> any  most
> I have hardly ~~some~~ time. It's like this ~~the most~~ days.

## some und any

■ **some** wird vor allem in bejahten Sätzen gebraucht, **any** (mit **not**) in verneinten.

I have **some** dollars but **not any** pounds.     I'd like **some more** time. I don't want **any help**.

**any** wird in Sätzen ohne **not** verwendet, wenn die Aussage negativ ist, ebenfalls in Sätzen mit **if**.

I'm **too tired** to do **any more** work. *... zu müde, um noch irgendwelche Arbeiten zu machen.*
We had **hardly any** customers so we **never** had **any** money. *... fast keine Kunden ... nie Geld.*
**If** we have **any** time, we can show the visitors round the factory. *Wenn wir etwas Zeit haben, ...*

■ In Fragen wird meist **any** gebraucht. **some** wird jedoch gebraucht, wenn man eine positive Antwort (**yes**) erwartet bzw. erhofft, insbesondere in Bitten und Angeboten.

Have you got **any** more information?     Can I have **some** paper, please?     Would you like **some** help?

■ Für **someone/somebody**, **something** usw. gelten die gleichen Regeln wie oben.

someone/somebody     something     somewhere
(not) anyone/anybody     (not) anything     (not) anywhere

## any in der Bedeutung „alle"/„jede(r/s)"

■ **any** hat auch die Bedeutung „jede(r/s) beliebige", **anybody** die Bedeutung „jeder", **anything** die Bedeutung „alles mögliche" oder „alles, egal was".

**Any** new product takes time to establish itself in the market. *Jedes neue Produkt ...*
**Anybody** in this department can make that decision. *Jeder in dieser Abteilung ...*
**Anything** could happen. *Es könnte alles passieren.*
I'll do **anything** you want. *Ich mache alles, was Sie wollen.*

## all – everybody/everyone – everything

■ Das deutsche „alle" im Sinne von „jedermann" wird meist mit **everybody/everyone** wiedergeben. „alles" entspricht **everything**.

**Everybody/Everyone** likes Tom. *Alle mögen Tom.*
**everybody/everyone** steht mit einem Verb in der Einzahl.
**Everything** is so expensive. *Alles ist so teuer.*

**!** **all** steht (als nachgestellter Teil des Subjekts in der Satzmitte) vor dem Vollverb, **nicht** dahinter.
They **all** speak English. (~~They speak all English.~~)

## most

**!** Vor **most** steht **kein the**.
**Most** (~~The most~~) people would like to have a lot of money. *Die meisten Menschen [überhaupt] ...*

Auf **most** kann **of + the** folgen, wenn von bestimmten Personen/Dingen gesprochen wird.
I know **most of the people** here. *Ich kenne die meisten [dieser bestimmten] Menschen hier.*

## **>** Das Wichtigste in Kürze

■ **some** in bejahten Sätzen, **any** in verneinten; in Fragen meist **any**; **some** in Bitten und Angeboten
■ „alle" = **everybody/everyone**; „alles" = **everything**
■ **all** steht vor einem Vollverb
■ Vor **most** **kein** ~~the~~

**A** **Underline the correct form.**

1  I haven't got **anything** / **something** to do.
2  I knew **most people** / **the most people** from a previous conference.
3  **All** / **Everything** is getting on my nerves at the moment.
4  Mark never has **any** / **some** time.
5  I have hardly **any** / **some** time this week.
6  I didn't see **anyone** / **someone** I knew at the conference.
7  My ex-colleagues **all came** / **came all** to my farewell party.
8  Can we start? **Are** / **Is** everybody here?

**B** **Complete with some/any, something/anything, someone/anyone or somewhere/anywhere.**

1  Martin never has ..................... sensible suggestions.

2  I'd like ................. fruit, but I can't see ................. in this breakfast buffet, not .................

3  Max is upset about ....................., I asked if I could help, but he wouldn't say .....................

4  You don't need to get ..................... more bottles of water, there are still ..................... left.

5  There was hardly ..................... from the marketing department at the meeting, and I didn't see
   ..................... from export sales either.

6  Have you got ..................... information for the next newsletter? I'd like to include
   ..................... about the new building.

7  Could you do ..................... for me? – Sure, but I don't have ..................... time just now.

8  I've phoned the office several times, but I can't get hold of ..................... There really doesn't
   seem to be ..................... there today.

9  I can't find my glasses ....................., but they must be here .....................

10  What time shall we meet tomorrow? – I'm busy in the morning, but am free all afternoon, so
    ..................... time then would be OK.

11  I haven't done ..................... all day. It's been wonderful!

**C** **Complete the sentences by ticking the correct position for all.**

1  I live in the centre, but my colleagues **A** [    ] live **B** [    ] further away.
2  We **A** [    ] work **B** [    ] really hard in our office.
3  The staff **A** [    ] left **B** [    ] the building **C** [    ] when the fire alarm rang.
4  The people in my office **A** [    ] have **B** [    ] been **C** [    ] on the training course.
5  You can ask anyone. **A** [    ] They **B** [    ] know **C** [    ] what to do.

**D** **Translate the following sentences.**

1  Ich würde alles tun, um eine neue Stelle zu finden.
2  Es ist schwierig, ein Hotelzimmer zu bekommen. Die meisten sind ausgebucht.
3  Wir haben die meisten Themen besprochen.
4  Meine Kollegen sprechen alle zwei Fremdsprachen.
5  Unser Chef hat kaum Papiere auf dem Schreibtisch.
6  Der Test war nicht schwer. Die meisten Fragen waren leicht zu beantworten.
7  Ich habe seit Monaten nichts von Tom gehört. Haben Sie etwas gehört?
8  Die meisten Leute hier haben viel Erfahrung.

> **I'll text     if I'm**
> ~~I text~~ you ~~when I'll be~~ late.

### Der Unterschied zwischen if und when = „wenn"

- In der Bedeutung „immer, wenn" / „jedes Mal, wenn" sind **when** und **if** austauschbar.
  **When**/**If** you do online banking, you need a password.

- In der Bedeutung „falls" muss „wenn" durch **if** wiedergegeben werden.
  **If** (~~When~~) it costs less, I'll go by train. *Wenn es weniger kostet, fahre ich mit dem Zug.*

### Was ist ein Bedingungsatz?

- In Bedingungssätzen wird gesagt, was unter bestimmten Voraussetzungen geschieht bzw. geschehen wird. Solche Sätze bestehen aus zwei Teilen.

  | **if**-Satz: nennt die Bedingung | Hauptsatz: nennt die Folge |
  | --- | --- |
  | **If** I have time today, | I'll write the minutes of the meeting. |
  | *Wenn ich heute Zeit habe,* | *schreibe ich das Protokoll der Sitzung.* |

  Der **if**-Satz kann hinter dem Hauptsatz stehen. In diesem Fall steht meist kein Komma dazwischen.
  Tom will call us **if** he needs our help. *Tom ruft uns, wenn er unsere Hilfe braucht.*

### Zeitenfolge in Bedingungssätzen des Typs 1

- Wenn **if** „immer, wenn" / „jedes Mal, wenn" bedeutet, steht in beiden Teilen (**if**-Satz und Hauptsatz) die einfache Gegenwart (**If** you **do** online banking, you **need** a password).

- Als Grundmuster gibt es jedoch in Bedingungssätzen des Typs 1 diese Zeitenfolge.

  | **if**-Satz: einfache Gegenwart | Hauptsatz: **will** |
  | --- | --- |
  | **If** Ann **finds** anything out, | she**'ll text** (~~she texts~~) us. |
  | *Wenn Ann etwas herausfindet,* | *schickt sie uns eine SMS.* |
  | **If** the weather **is** bad, | we**'ll** probably **stay** overnight. |
  | *Wenn das Wetter schlecht ist,* | *bleiben wir wahrscheinlich über Nacht.* |

### Abweichungen vom Grundmuster im if-Satz

- Im **if**-Satz kann auch die Verlaufsform oder ein Modalverb wie **can, must, should** usw. stehen.
  **If** I **am driving**, I **won't take** any calls. *Wenn ich gerade am Fahren bin, werde ich keine Anrufe annehmen.*
  **If** you **can't do** it, I'll **do** it myself. *Wenn Sie es nicht machen können, mache ich es selbst.*

**!** Als Faustregel gilt: **kein will** im **if**-Satz: **If** I **am** (~~will be~~) late, I'll phone.

Ausnahme: wenn **will** deutsch „wollen" entspricht und eine Bitte oder einen verdeckten Befehl ausdrückt.
**If** you**'ll** please **sign** here, … *Wenn Sie hier bitte unterschreiben wollen, …*

### Abweichungen vom Grundmuster im Hauptsatz

- Im Hauptsatz kann neben **will** auch eine Befehlsform, ein Modalverb oder auch **going to** stehen.
  **If** he's really that good, **hire** him. *Wenn er wirklich so gut ist, stell ihn ein.*
  **If** we book early, we **can save** money. *Wenn wir früh buchen, können wir Geld sparen.*
  **If** it's not too expensive, I**'m going to buy** it. *Wenn es nicht zu teuer ist, will ich es kaufen.*

> ### Das Wichtigste in Kürze
> - „wenn" im zeitlichen Sinne = **when**; „wenn" im Sinne von „falls" = **if**
> - Grundmuster: **if**-Satz: Gegenwartsform – Hauptsatz: **will**
> - **Kein** ~~will~~ im **if**-Satz (außer bei Bitten)

Weitere Informationen → Units 45, 46

**A** **Underline the correct form.**

1 If you **see** / **will see** Martin, will you ask him for a copy of the contract, please?
2 **If** / **When** the goods don't arrive today, we will have real problems.
3 I **am not able** / **won't be able** to meet the deadline if I don't start soon.
4 Mark will be annoyed if we **don't** / **won't** keep him informed.
5 If you're still discussing item 7, **I'll go away** / **I go away** and come back later.

**B** **Which sentence is correct?**

1 **A** I'm not sad when this project will be over.
  **B** I won't be sad when this project is over.

2 **A** If Kevin doesn't manage to contact Mr Li, we'll make alternative plans.
  **B** If Kevin won't manage to contact Mr Li, we make alternative plans.

3 **A** If demand increases and supply remains the same, prices rise.
  **B** If demand will increase and supply will remain the same, prices rise.

**C** **Make sentences using the basic pattern (if-clause: simple present; main clause: will).**

1 If the taxi / not come soon, we / miss our train. ...............................................................

2 We / break for lunch soon if that / be OK with you. ...............................................................

3 What / you / do if your boss / not let you take time off? ...............................................................

4 If I / not finish this today, I / come in early tomorrow. ...............................................................

5 If you / get the coffee, I / make the photocopies. ...............................................................

**D** **Complete these dialogues.**

1 A: When do you have to leave for the airport?

  B: Well, if I ......................... (take) a taxi, I ......................... (be able to) leave a bit later.

2 A: When are you going to send Manila the paperwork?

  B: It ......................... (should) be early enough if I ......................... (email) it tomorrow.

3 A: I've forgotten to invite that new person to our jour fixe. What's her name?

  B: Maja. I haven't invited her either, but of course if we ......................... (not tell) her about it,

  she ......................... (not know) that it's taking place.

4 A: Are we going to order from Thailand again?

  B: I don't know. If you ......................... (think) it's a good idea, we .........................

  (could) try out that company in Malaysia.

**E** **Translate the following sentences.**

1 Wenn er nicht bald kommt, fangen wir ohne ihn an.
2 Was machen Sie, wenn der Streik nicht am Freitag vorbei ist?
3 Gehst du zum Seminar, wenn der Chef dich lässt?
4 Wenn Sie einen Augenblick warten wollen, schaue ich, was ich tun kann.
5 Wir wollen die polnische Maschine kaufen, wenn wir nicht ein besseres Angebot bekommen.
6 Wenn Tom die Stelle nicht bekommt, wird er sehr enttäuscht sein.

> **would be     didn't have to**
> Everything ~~were~~ great if I ~~wouldn't have to~~ work this weekend.

### Bedingungssätze des Typs 2: „Was wäre, wenn …"

■ In dem folgenden if-Satz des Typs 1 wird eine Situation beschrieben, die durchaus möglich ist.
If we can resolve the last point, we'll be able to complete the negotiations today.
*Wenn wir den letzten Punkt klären können, werden wir heute die Verhandlungen abschließen können.*
Der Sprecher sieht es als vorstellbar, vielleicht sogar wahrscheinlich an, dass eine Einigung heute erreicht wird.

■ Der folgende if-Satz beschreibt eine Situation, die unwahrscheinlich oder sogar unmöglich ist.
If they reduced their price by 90 %, I would buy.
*Wenn sie ihren Preis um 90 % reduzieren würden, würde ich kaufen.*
Der Sprecher hält es für unwahrscheinlich oder unmöglich, dass der Preis um 90 % reduziert wird. Er fantasiert, stellt sich vor, unter welchen Bedingungen er kaufen würde. Er spricht darüber, was wäre, wenn die Dinge anders lägen. Diese Art von Bedingungssatz wird als Typ 2 bezeichnet.

### Zeitenfolge in Bedingungssätzen des Typs 2

■ Als Grundmuster gibt es in Bedingungssätzen des Typs 2 diese Zeitenfolge.

| if-Satz: einfache Vergangenheit | Hauptsatz: would/could/might + Infinitiv |
|---|---|
| If I **knew** the answer, | **I'd** (= I **would**) **tell** you. |
| *Wenn ich die Antwort wüsste,* | *würde ich sie Ihnen sagen.* |
| If we **lived** in Australia, | we **could spend** Christmas on the beach. |
| *Wenn wir in Australien lebten,* | *könnten wir Weihnachten am Strand verbringen.* |
| If the conference **was** in a nicer place, | I **might go**. |
| *Wenn die Tagung an einem schöneren Ort wäre,* | *würde ich vielleicht teilnehmen.* |

 Im if-Satz steht die Vergangenheitsform – der Satz bezieht sich aber auf die Gegenwart/Zukunft.

 Als Faustregel gilt: **kein** would im if-Satz: If I **won** (~~would win~~) a million dollars, I'd travel round the world.

### Abweichungen vom Grundmuster im if-Satz

■ Im if-Satz ist would möglich, wenn eine Bitte oder ein verdeckter Befehl ausgedrückt wird.
If you **would sign** here, I could get the shipment on its way this week.
*Wenn Sie hier unterschreiben würden, könnte ich die Sendung diese Woche noch auf den Weg bringen.*

■ Im if-Satz kann auch die Verlaufsform der Vergangenheit oder ein Modalverb stehen.
If you **were interviewing** me, what questions would you ask? *Wenn Sie mich interviewen würden, …*
If I **couldn't pay** by credit card, I would have to change money. *Wenn ich nicht … bezahlen könnte, …*

### if I were you

■ if I were you entspricht „an deiner/eurer/Ihrer Stelle".
If **I were you**, I'd book early. *An Ihrer Stelle würde ich frühzeitig buchen.*
I wouldn't wait if **I were you**. *An Ihrer Stelle würde ich nicht warten.*

### Das Wichtigste in Kürze
■ if-Satz: einfache Vergangenheit – Hauptsatz: would/could/might + Infinitiv
■ Kein ~~would~~ im if-Satz (außer bei Bitten und verdeckten Befehlen)

**A** Underline the correct form.

1 I would help you, if I **had** / **would have** the time.
2 What **did you do** / **would you do** if you were offered a job in Hong Kong?
3 If I were you, I **didn't accept** / **wouldn't accept** a change in contract.
4 If I could help you, I **will** / **would** do so gladly.

**B** Which sentence is correct?

1 **A** If we asked for another two weeks, they wouldn't agree.
  **B** If we would ask for another two weeks, they didn't agree.

2 **A** If you had the chance, would you go on the management training scheme?
  **B** If you would have the chance, would you go on the management training scheme?

3 **A** The banks might lend us the money if we made a better business plan.
  **B** The banks might lend us the money if we would make a better business plan.

4 **A** If I could afford it, I would ask to reduce my working hours.
  **B** If I would be able to afford it, I asked to reduce my working hours.

5 **A** If you would fill in this form, that would be a great help.
  **B** If you would fill in this form, that were a great help.

**C** Make sentences using **would** in the main clause.

1 Why do you work so hard? If you / work less, you / not have so many health problems.
2 I don't understand why Martin spends so much time writing emails. If he / talk on the phone more often, he / be able to save quite a bit of time.
3 Have you seen this job ad? It sounds really interesting. If I / be you, I / apply for it.
4 Jim's often late for work. If he / be more punctual, he / probably get on better with his boss.
5 Why do you always order from the same company? If you / try some other companies, I'm sure you / get a better price.

**D** Make complete sentences. Use conditional 1 or 2.

1 I'm sure it will never happen, but if I / win a lot of money, I / not give up my job.
2 Don't book a hotel. You / can stay with us if you / want to.
3 You like Italian food, don't you? If it / be not too late, I / try and book a table at Da Marco for this evening.
4 If I / be you, I / check with the boss before signing.
5 If I / not get round to calling you this evening, I / do it tomorrow – I promise.
6 Thank goodness we have Dores in the department. If we / not have a Portuguese speaker, doing business with that company in Porto / be much more difficult.

**E** Translate the following sentences.

1 An Ihrer Stelle würde ich nicht am Wochenende reisen.
2 Ich würde Ihnen helfen, wenn ich nicht um 14.00 Uhr eine Sitzung hätte.
3 Wenn ich nicht mehrere Male umsteigen müsste, würde ich mit öffentlichen Verkehrsmitteln zur Arbeit fahren.
4 Maxine würde sich um die Stelle bewerben, wenn Robert nicht in der Abteilung arbeiten würde.
5 Wenn wir nicht immer in jenem grässlichen Hotel Montador wohnen müssten, würde ich gern zur Messe fahren.
6 Wenn Sie die Papiere ein paar Tage vor unserem Treffen schicken würden, wäre das hilfreich.

<u>hadn't been</u>                                        <u>wouldn't have missed</u>

If there ~~wouldn't been~~ an accident on the road to the airport, I ~~hadn't missed~~ my plane.

### Bedingungssätze des Typs 3: „Was wäre damals gewesen, wenn …"

- In den folgenden if-Sätzen wird eine vergangene Situation beschrieben, die sich nicht so ereignet hat.
  If I had left the office earlier, I would have got to the airport in time.
  *Wenn ich das Büro früher verlassen hätte, wäre ich rechtzeitig zum Flughafen gekommen.*
  **Realität: Ich habe das Büro nicht früher verlassen.**

  If we had had enough time, we would have visited the old city.
  *Wenn wir genug Zeit gehabt hätten, hätten wir die Altstadt besucht.*
  **Realität: Wir hatten nicht genug Zeit.**

  **Die beschriebene Situation war nie Wirklichkeit und kann es auch nicht werden, weil sie der abgeschlossenen Vergangenheit angehört. Der Sprecher stellt sich aber vor, was gewesen wäre. Diese Art von Bedingungssatz wird als Typ 3 bezeichnet.**

### Zeitenfolge in Bedingungssätzen des Typs 3

- Als Grundmuster gibt es in Bedingungssätzen des Typs 3 diese Zeitenfolge.

  | if-Satz: Past Perfect | Hauptsatz: would/could/might + have + Partizip Perfekt |
  |---|---|
  | If I **had seen** Ann, | I **would have told** her the good news. |
  | *Wenn ich Ann gesehen hätte,* | *hätte ich ihr die gute Nachricht erzählt.* |
  | If you **had been** more open, | we **could have avoided** misunderstandings. |
  | *Wenn Sie offener gewesen wären,* | *hätten wir Missverständnisse vermeiden können.* |
  | If we **had asked** Tony, | he **might have helped** us. |
  | *Wenn wir Tony gefragt hätten,* | *hätte er uns vielleicht geholfen.* |

- Oft werden verneinte Formen gebraucht.
  I **wouldn't have called** you if it **hadn't been** so urgent.
  *Ich hätte Sie nicht angerufen, wenn es nicht so dringend gewesen wäre.*
  If I **had arrived** the night before, I **wouldn't have been** so tired.
  *Wenn ich am Vorabend angereist wäre, wäre ich nicht so müde gewesen.*

### Mischformen von Bedingungssätzen des Typs 2 und 3

- Die Zeitenfolge in Bedingungssätzen des Typs 2 und 3 kann auch eine Mischung der beiden Grundmuster darstellen. Es gibt zwei Möglichkeiten.

  | 1. if-Satz: Simple Past | Hauptsatz: would/could/might + have + Partizip Perfekt |
  |---|---|
  | If I **spoke** Spanish, | I **would have understood** Pedro's question. |
  | *Wenn ich Spanisch sprechen würde,* | *hätte ich Pedros Frage verstanden.* |

  | 2. if-Satz: Past Perfect | Hauptsatz: would/could/might + Infinitiv |
  |---|---|
  | If I **hadn't taken** the wrong road, | we **would be** there now. |
  | *Wenn ich mich nicht verfahren hätte,* | *wären wir jetzt schon da.* |

> ### Das Wichtigste in Kürze
> - if-Satz: Past Perfect – Hauptsatz: would/could/might + have + Partizip Perfekt
> - Mischformen:
>   if-Satz: Simple Past – Hauptsatz: would/could/might + have + Partizip Perfekt
>   if-Satz: Past Perfect – Hauptsatz: would/could/might + Infinitiv

Weitere Informationen ⟶ Units 44, 45

**A** **Underline the correct form.**

**1** I **had got** / **would have got** more dollars if I had exchanged my euros last week.

**2** If the price **had fallen** / **would have fallen** a bit more, I would have bought more.

**3** What **had you done** / **would you have done** if the flight had been cancelled?

**4** If I **had known** / **would have known** about this earlier, I wouldn't have made the offer.

**5** If I knew the answer, I **hadn't asked** / **wouldn't have asked** you.

**B** **Which sentence is correct?**

**1** **A** If I'd known you were on the same flight, we could have shared a taxi.
   **B** If I knew you were on the same flight, we could have shared a taxi.

**2** **A** I wouldn't have been late for work if I didn't forget to set my alarm clock.
   **B** I wouldn't have been late for work if I hadn't forgotten to set my alarm clock.

**3** **A** The banks might have lent us the money if we had made a better business plan.
   **B** The banks might lend us the money if we would have made a better business plan.

**4** **A** If we would have bought the machine last year, it had been cheaper.
   **B** If we had bought the machine last year, it would have been cheaper.

**5** **A** If the airport hadn't been closed, we wouldn't have had to drive all the way.
   **B** If the airport hadn't been closed, we didn't have to drive all the way.

**6** **A** It's good to be here at last. If Max hadn't given me a lift, I'd probably still be in the taxi queue.
   **B** It's good to be here at last. If Max hadn't given me a lift, I were probably still in the taxi queue.

**7** **A** If there hadn't been so many interruptions, I might have finished this work yesterday.
   **B** If there weren't so many interruptions, I would finish this work yesterday.

**C** **Make complete type 3 sentences.**

**1** Everywhere was booked, but Mark found us something. If he / not have the right connections, we / not get a room. ...................................................................................................

**2** I don't know why you didn't apply for that job last month. I'm sure you / get it if you / apply.
...................................................................................................

**3** The management didn't increase their offer. The workers / not go on strike if the management / agree to pay them more. ...................................................................................................

**4** All flights were cancelled. We / not have a video conference if the weather / not force us to change our plans. ...................................................................................................

**5** Jane had no idea about the company's financial problems when she accepted a job there. She / take the job if she / know. ...................................................................................................

**6** Dave lost his passport. If someone / not find it in the street, he / be in real trouble.
...................................................................................................

**D** **Translate the following sentences.**

**1** Wenn ich nicht so viel Gepäck gehabt hätte, wäre ich zu Fuß zum Bahnhof gegangen.

**2** Wenn wir gewusst hätten, wie teuer Alkohol ist, hätten wir etwas anderes getrunken.

**3** Wenn du nicht gekommen wärst und mich mitgenommen hättest *(give a lift)* , hätte ich die Sitzung verpasst.

**4** All dies wäre nicht passiert, wenn Sie sorgfältiger gearbeitet hätten.

**5** Wenn wir diese Entscheidung früher gefällt hätten, wäre die Situation nicht so dramatisch.

**6** Wenn ich Mr Li kennen würde, hätte ich die E-Mail an ihn geschrieben.

---

New mail

To:

*said that / told me that*        *had found*

Mr Li ~~said me that~~ he expects to reach a decision soon and that he ~~has found~~ the meeting useful.

---

### Direkte Rede – Indirekte Rede

- Was jemand sagt, kann man direkt (wörtlich, als Zitat) wiedergeben oder indirekt „berichten".
  Direkte Rede:     Amy said, **"Pavel is an expert."** *Amy sagte: „Pavel ist ein Experte".*
  Indirekte Rede:    Amy said **that Pavel was an expert**. *Amy sagte, Pavel sei/wäre ein Experte.*

Die indirekte Rede leitet man meist mit **say** oder **tell** ein. Nach **tell** nennt man die Person, der etwas gesagt wurde. Wird die Person nicht genannt, so muss **say** verwendet werden.
He **told me** (~~told~~) that he knows London well. / He **said** (~~said me~~) that he knows London well.

Vor **that** darf **kein** Komma stehen – **that** wird aber oft auch weggelassen.
Tony **said that** (~~said, that~~) he will be here at six.    Ann **said she** (~~said, that she~~) doesn't have the address.

### Zeitverschiebung in der indirekten Rede

- Steht das einleitende Verb der indirekten Rede in der Vergangenheit (z. B. **said**), so wird eine Gegenwartsform im berichteten Satz in die Vergangenheit „verschoben". Das gilt für Vollverb und Hilfsverb.

| Gegenwart | | ⋯⟩ Vergangenheit |
|---|---|---|
| **Vollverb** | "I **feel** great." | ⋯⟩ She said (that) she **felt** great. |
| **Hilfsverb be** (Verlaufsform) | "I'm **working** hard." | ⋯⟩ She said (that) she **was** working hard. |
| **Hilfsverb be** (be going to) | "I'm **going** to stay." | ⋯⟩ She said (that) she **was** going to stay. |
| **Hilfsverb have** (Present Perfect) | "I've **had** problems." | ⋯⟩ She said (that) she **had** had problems. |
| **Hilfsverb will** (Zukunft) | "I'll **be** there." | ⋯⟩ She said (that) she **would** be there. |
| **Hilfsverb can** | "I **can/may** come." | ⋯⟩ She said (that) she **could/might** come. |

- Ein Verb in der Vergangenheit kann, muss aber nicht „verschoben" werden.

| Vergangenheit | | ⋯⟩ Vergangenheit oder Past Perfect |
|---|---|---|
| **Vollverb** | "We **spoke** to Ed." | ⋯⟩ She said (that) they **spoke** / **had spoken** to Ed. |
| **Hilfsverb be** (Verlaufsform) | "He **was** travelling." | ⋯⟩ She said (that) he **was** / **had been** travelling. |

- Das Hilfsverb **had** (zur Bildung des Past Perfect) und die Modalverben **could** (= könnte), **might**, **should** und **would** bleiben unverändert.

| **Hilfsverb had** (Past Perfect) | "I **had** already eaten." | ⋯⟩ She said (that) she **had** already eaten. |
|---|---|---|
| **could/might** | "It **could/might** happen." | ⋯⟩ She said (that) it **could/might** happen. |
| **should** | "We **should** wait." | ⋯⟩ She said (that) we **should** wait. |
| **would** | "Ed **wouldn't** agree." | ⋯⟩ She said (that) Ed **wouldn't** agree. |

- Eine Zeitverschiebung muss nicht stattfinden, wenn das Berichtete immer oder immer noch gilt.
  "I **hate** this building." ⋯⟩ She said (that) she **hates/hated** this building.

Man wählt aber bewusst die Zeitverschiebung, wenn man sich von dem, was man berichtet, distanzieren und zeigen will, dass man dessen Wahrheitsgehalt nicht garantiert oder garantieren kann.
Politiker:        Zeitungsbericht:
"Inflation **is** low."    The government said that inflation **was** low.

---

> ### Das Wichtigste in Kürze
> - Einleitendes Verb: **tell** + Person; **say** nur ohne Person
> - Zeitverschiebung bei einleitendem Verb in der Vergangenheit: Gegenwart ⋯⟩ Vergangenheit

### A  Which sentence is correct?

**1** **A** Tom told me he had seen Mark Thompson on the train.
   **B** Tom told he had seen Mark Thompson on the train.

**2** **A** Jane said me she had had a good meeting.
   **B** Jane said she had had a good meeting.

**3** **A** The trainer told us, that in some countries people avoid eye contact.
   **B** The trainer told us that in some countries people avoid eye contact.

**4** **A** Max told me over an hour ago that you have arrived. Why didn't you report to me?
   **B** Max told me over an hour ago that you had arrived. Why didn't you report to me?

**5** **A** "I'm meeting Ms Salomon." ⋯⟩ Mr Foster said he met Ms Salomon.
   **B** "I'm meeting Ms Salomon." ⋯⟩ Mr Foster said he was meeting Ms Salomon.

**6** **A** "I want to be at the presentation." ⋯⟩ Martha said she would be at the presentation.
   **B** "I want to be at the presentation." ⋯⟩ Martha said she wanted to be at the presentation.

**7** **A** "We're going to need more time." ⋯⟩ Jonas said they would be going to need more time.
   **B** "We're going to need more time." ⋯⟩ Jonas said they were going to need more time.

### B  Put the following sentences into indirect speech.

"I don't want to go to Spain again." ⋯⟩ Sandra explained that *she didn't want to go to Spain again*.

**1** "I can help and Pedro may have time too." ⋯⟩ Frank is so unreliable. Yesterday he promised he
..................................... and said Pedro ........................................, but then
they left me to do everything myself!
**2** "We've leased the cars. It will be better for the company's cashflow." ⋯⟩ When I spoke to Bruno he told
me they ........................................ He said ...............................................
**3** "You'll have to work harder if you want to get a bonus." ⋯⟩ My colleague told me I .....................
........................................................................ . I did work harder, but
then they cancelled all bonuses for twelve months.
**4** "The situation is critical and I don't want to make any mistakes." ⋯⟩ At the height of the crisis Mr Poynton
explained that ................................... and ...........................................
**5** "I've had two job interviews, but I'm not really interested in either of the jobs." ⋯⟩ Tom said he ..........
.......................................................... So he's still looking.

### C  Report the following things which you have heard through office gossip and don't really believe.

**1** "They're going to employ a stress counsellor." ⋯⟩ Someone in the personnel department apparently said
that they ...............................................................................................
**2** "Costs rose by 8%." ⋯⟩ One of the managers claimed that ...............................................
**3** "They have decided to merge the two departments." ⋯⟩ One anxious colleague said that ................
.......................................................................
**4** "Mr Aikens has been offered a job by Domicks Ltd and is leaving." ⋯⟩ At the conference there was a
rumour that ............................................................................................

### D  Complete this report. Change the direct speech verbs in brackets into reported speech.

The CEO said that one thing (**"is"**) ..........[1] clear: the crisis (**"has transformed"**) ......................[2]
the world and the environment in which companies (**"do"**) ..............[3] business. The role of the state,
in particular, (**"has changed"**) ........................[4]. She said that everybody (**"has"**) ..............[5]
great admiration for the way in which governments (**"prevented"**) ......................[6] a break-down of
the whole system, but there (**"is"**) ...........[7] a real danger that the changed role of the state (**"will
open"**) ......................[8] the door to isolationism and protectionism. She said that we (**"don't yet
know"**) ........................[9] if policymakers (**"will be able to"**) ...........................[10] avoid
this danger.

We asked him where ~~he did study~~ *he studied* and what qualifications ~~did he have~~ *he had*.

**Fragen in der indirekten Rede**

■ Entscheidungsfragen leitet man mit ask + if/whether (= ob) ein. Nach ask steht kein Komma.
Die Zeiten der direkten Rede werden „verschoben" wie in Aussagesätzen (siehe Unit 47).
"**Is** the machine working?" ⋯⟩ He **asked if/whether** the machine **was** working. *Er fragte, ob ... funktionierte.*
"**Can** you see?" ⋯⟩ He **asked if/whether** I **could** see. *Er fragte, ob ich sehen könn(t)e.*

**!** do/does/did erscheint in der indirekten Frage nicht.
"**Do** you **know** Mr Li?" ⋯⟩ He **asked if/whether** I **knew** Mr Li.
"**Did** Petra **go** to the restaurant?" ⋯⟩ He **asked if/whether** Petra **had gone** to the restaurant.

■ wh-Fragen leitet man mit ask + Fragewort ein.
"**Where**'s Max?" ⋯⟩ He **asked where** Max was.
"**Who** have you spoken to?" ⋯⟩ He **asked who** I had spoken to.

■ Auch Ausdrücke wie want to know / find out / wonder können die indirekte Rede einleiten.
"**Who**'s coming?" ⋯⟩ He **wanted to know / wanted to find out / wondered** who was coming.

**Bitten und Befehle in der indirekten Rede**

■ Bitten gibt man mit ask somebody (not) to do something wieder.
"I'd like some help, please." ⋯⟩ Martin **asked me to help** him. *Martin bat mich, ihm zu helfen.*
"Please don't wait for me." ⋯⟩ Julia **asked me not to wait** for her. *Julia bat mich, nicht auf sie zu warten.*

■ Befehle gibt man mit tell somebody (not) to do something wieder.
"Leave us alone." ⋯⟩ Ann **told me to leave** them alone. *Ann sagte mir, dass ich sie allein lassen sollte.*
"Don't do it." ⋯⟩ Ed **told me not to do** it. *Ed sagte mir, dass ich es nicht tun sollte.*

**Orts- und Zeitbestimmungen in der indirekten Rede**

Berichtet man etwas an einem anderen Ort bzw. nachdem ein bestimmter Zeitraum vorbei ist,
so muss man bestimmte Orts- und Zeitbestimmungen der direkten Rede anders wiedergeben.
"Tom's not **here**." ⋯⟩ He said Tom wasn't **there**.
"I can't come **today**." ⋯⟩ He said he couldn't come **that day**.
"I met Bill **yesterday**." ⋯⟩ He said he had met Bill **the day before**.
"We're leaving **tomorrow**." ⋯⟩ He said they were leaving **the next day**.
"The fair is **this week/month/year**." ⋯⟩ He said the fair was **that week/month/year**.
"Ed died **last Sunday/week/month/year**." ⋯⟩ He said Ed had died **the Sunday/week/month/year before**.
"I'm moving **next Monday/week ...**" ⋯⟩ He said he was moving **the following Monday/week/...**

**!** Ist ein genannter Zeitraum noch nicht abgeschlossen, bleibt die Zeitbestimmung erhalten.
(March) "We should make a profit **this year**."
(June) In March you said that we should make a profit **this year**.

**Das Wichtigste in Kürze**

■ Indirekte Fragen: ask + if/whether oder ask + Fragewort
■ Indirekte Bitten/Befehle: ask/tell somebody (not) to do something
■ here ⋯⟩ there; today ⋯⟩ that day; yesterday ⋯⟩ the day before; tomorrow ⋯⟩ the next day;
this ... ⋯⟩ that ... ; last ... ⋯⟩ the ... before; next ... ⋯⟩ the following ...

Weitere Informationen → Unit 47

**A** **Which sentence is correct?**

**1** **A** Tom asked me if I did know how long Sandra had been with the company.
   **B** Tom asked me if I knew how long Sandra had been with the company.

**2** **A** One of the guests was wandering about in the corridor and asked me where the toilet was.
   **B** One of the guests was wandering about in the corridor and asked me where was the toilet.

**3** **A** "Is Sue coming?" ····⟩ Jane asked me, if Sue was coming.
   **B** "Is Sue coming?" ····⟩ Jane asked me if Sue was coming.

**4** **A** "Can you come a bit earlier?" ····⟩ My boss asked us to come a bit earlier.
   **B** "Can you come a bit earlier?" ····⟩ My boss said us to come a bit earlier.

**B** **Report the following requests and commands.**

**1** "Meet me outside the hotel." **(Tony/Maria)** Tony told Maria ....................................
**2** "Don't wait, start the presentation." **(My boss / me)** ..........................................
**3** "Can you help me, please?" **(Mrs Chan / Colin)** ..............................................
**4** "Don't be late." **(Mrs Williams / Philip)** ..................................................
**5** "Could you look at page 4?" **(The presenter / us)** ............................................
**6** "Speak more slowly." **(trainer/participant)** The trainer ......................................

**C** **Report these sentences.**

**1** Rodrigo: "I'm getting a new boss and she's starting next week."
   I spoke to Rodrigo at least two months ago, and he told me then ............................
   ....................................................................................

**2** Ed: "Angela and I are going to Beijing next month."
   Last year some time Ed said ......................................................................,
   but the trip was cancelled.

**3** Carol: "Adrian's not normally late and I'm sure he will be here soon."
   Carol said Adrian ................................................................................
   .............................., but he was in fact ill.

**4** Joanna: "I had an interview yesterday and I expect to hear something by the end of this week."
   When I saw Joanna two weeks ago she told me ..............................................
   ....................................................................................
   But I think she's still heard nothing.

**5** Markus: "I'm moving office tomorrow, but they still haven't told me where to!"
   When I last spoke to Markus he said ..........................................................
   ....................................................................................

**D** **Report these questions.**

**1** The personnel manager: "Did you understand Mr Taylor's question?"
   The personnel manager asked me ..........................................................

**2** Samantha: "What time of year does the Hanover Fair usually take place?"
   Samantha wanted to know ................................................................

**3** Marek: "Why am I not being invited?"
   For weeks before the conference Marek kept asking ......................................

**4** Jane: "When is Mr Li flying back?"
   Jane wanted to know ....................................................................

**5** Line manager: "Can you work next Saturday?"
   About a month ago my line manager asked me ............................................
   ................... I said 'yes', but he didn't give me any time off to make up for it.

**6** Tom: "Where is everyone meeting up this evening?"
   On the first day of the seminar Tom asked ..............................................

# 1 Simple present and present progressive

**A** Fill in **is, isn't, are, aren't, do, does, don't** or **doesn't**. There is one word that you don't need.

**1** A: We ............... having the presentation in this room. It's too small and it ............... have

enough chairs.

B: How many people ............... you expecting?

**2** A: ............... Frank know that Max is away and ............... coming

to the meeting?

**3** A: ............... Mr Li and Shuna speak German?

B: No, they ..............., only English.

Points /7

**B** Underline the correct form.

**1** I **am not seeing** / **don't see** where we can make further savings.

**2** We used the agency once before. **Aren't you remembering?** / **Don't you remember?**

**3** We **are thinking** / **think** of moving the launch date back a month.

**4** What **are they all laughing about** / **do they all laugh about**? Have I done something stupid?

**5** What **are you having** / **do you have**? Coffee, water? Or can I get you some juice?

**6** Marianne **has** / **is having** no employees – she's a one-woman business.

**7** **Is anyone using** / **Does anyone use** the conference room today, do you know?

**8** **Does this figure include** / **Is this figure including** the development costs?

Points /8

**C** Complete with the correct simple present or present progressive form.

**1** I ....................... (go) back to the hotel now. ..................................... (anybody/want)

to share a taxi with me?

**2** Emma ....................... (still wait for) her visa.

**3** Hi, it's me. I ....................... (phone) to say that I ....................... (work) from home today.

**4** Henrietta ....................... (not like) our new boss.

**5** The conference is better than last year, isn't it? ..................................... (you/enjoy) it?

**6** Sorry, Lena ....................... (speak) to a client on the other line. Can she call you back?

**7** There's a supply shortage just now and prices ....................... (rise).

**8** ..................................... (our partners / still think) about how to respond?

**9** ..................................... (you/realize) how much it's all going to cost?

**10** The decision ....................... (not mean) that the whole project is stopped.

**11** Why ..................................... (you all / look) at me like that?

Points /15

**12** When you plan a project like this, how much time ....................... (you/include) for quality testing?

**13** I'm sorry. I ....................... (owe) you an apology.

Total Points /30

# TEST

## 2 Simple past and present perfect

**A** **Complete with the correct simple past form.**

Last Tuesday I . . . . . . . . . . . . . . . . . . . . .[1] **(fly)** to Lisbon on business. I . . . . . . . . . . . . . . . . . . . . .[2] **(not stay)** in

a hotel, but with friends. I . . . . . . . . . . . . . . . . . . . . .[3] **(try)** to invite them out for a meal, but they

. . . . . . . . . . . . . . . . . . . . .[4] **(not have)** any time on the only evening that I . . . . . . . . . . . . . . . . . . . . .[5] **(be)** free.

So I . . . . . . . . . . . . . . . . . . . . .[6] **(buy)** two tickets for a Latin American music festival next month and

. . . . . . . . . . . . . . . . . . . . .[7] **(leave)** them on the bed with a note. I . . . . . . . . . . . . . . . . . . . . .[8] **(pay)** quite a lot

for them, but I . . . . . . . . . . . . . . . . . . . . .[9] **(spend)** nothing on food or accommodation all week.

Points
☐ /9

**B** **Make sentences. There are always one or two words that you don't need.**

was / you / Where / born? / were ⟶ **Where were you born?**

1  at the event. / didn't / anyone from the Luxembourg office / saw / see / We

. . . . . . . . . . . . . . . . . . . . . . . . . . . . . . . . . . . . . . . . . . . . . . . . . . . . . . . . . . . . . . . . . . . . . . . . . . . . . . . . . . . . . . . . . . . . . .

2  fell / felt / Prices / quite sharply.

. . . . . . . . . . . . . . . . . . . . . . . . . . . . . . . . . . . . . . . . . . . . . . . . . . . . . . . . . . . . . . . . . . . . . . . . . . . . . . . . . . . . . . . . . . . . . .

3  did / for your hotel? / paid / payed / Who

. . . . . . . . . . . . . . . . . . . . . . . . . . . . . . . . . . . . . . . . . . . . . . . . . . . . . . . . . . . . . . . . . . . . . . . . . . . . . . . . . . . . . . . . . . . . . .

4  be / didn't / expensive. / The hotel / wasn't

. . . . . . . . . . . . . . . . . . . . . . . . . . . . . . . . . . . . . . . . . . . . . . . . . . . . . . . . . . . . . . . . . . . . . . . . . . . . . . . . . . . . . . . . . . . . . .

5  a very good time last night. / didn't / hadn't / have / We

. . . . . . . . . . . . . . . . . . . . . . . . . . . . . . . . . . . . . . . . . . . . . . . . . . . . . . . . . . . . . . . . . . . . . . . . . . . . . . . . . . . . . . . . . . . . . .

6  nobody from the export department available / so I / speak / spoke / to the marketing manager. /

There / was / were

. . . . . . . . . . . . . . . . . . . . . . . . . . . . . . . . . . . . . . . . . . . . . . . . . . . . . . . . . . . . . . . . . . . . . . . . . . . . . . . . . . . . . . . . . . . . . .

7  didn't / said. / Sorry, I / not / understand / understood / what / you

. . . . . . . . . . . . . . . . . . . . . . . . . . . . . . . . . . . . . . . . . . . . . . . . . . . . . . . . . . . . . . . . . . . . . . . . . . . . . . . . . . . . . . . . . . . . . .

Points
☐ /7

**C** **Complete with the correct present perfect form.**

1  I . . . . . . . . . . . . . . . . . . . . . . . . . . . . . . . . . . . . **(try)** to persuade Michael to join us, but he doesn't want to.

2  We . . . . . . . . . . . . . . . . . . . . . . . . . . . . . . **(not make)** much progress so far.

3  I emailed Mr Li yesterday, but he still . . . . . . . . . . . . . . . . . . . . . . . . . . . . . . . . . . . . **(not reply)**.

4  . . . . . . . . . . . . . . . . . . . . . . . . . . . . . . **(you/hear)** the news?

5  We . . . . . . . . . . . . . . . . . . . . . . . . . . . . **(already sell)** more than last year.

6  I . . . . . . . . . . . . . . . . . . . . . . . . . . . . . . **(lose)** track of where we are on this project.

7  The phone . . . . . . . . . . . . . . . . . . . . . . . . . . . . . . . . . . . . **(not stop)** ringing all day!

8  I . . . . . . . . . . . . . . . . . . . . . . . . . . . . . . **(write)** to them three times.

Points
☐ /8

**D** Circle the right answer.

1  I ... the Philippines. What's it like?

   **A** didn't ever be in  **B** have never been to  **C** have been never in  **D** never was in

2  ... Mr Baroso? He's here for the conference.

   **A** Do you meet  **B** Did you met  **C** Have you meet  **D** Have you met

3  We still ... a suitable replacement for Diana Prestel.

   **A** don't find  **B** didn't found  **C** haven't found  **D** haven't founded

4  I've only just heard the news. When ... about this?

   **A** did you hear  **B** did you heard  **C** has you heard  **D** have you heard

5  You ... in Brandenburg if I remember rightly. Is that so?

   **A** are born  **B** have been born  **C** was born  **D** were born

6  It's not the most pleasant task, I know. I ... many times.

   **A** do it  **B** did do it  **C** done it  **D** have done it

7  Mike attended the presentation for us. He ... Ann Miles there.

   **A** have saw  **B** have seen  **C** saw  **D** seen

Points

/8

8  Ronaldo ... ill for two days, but was back on the stand for the last day of the fair.

   **A** has been  **B** have been  **C** was  **D** were

**E** Correct the mistake.

1  ~~Soraya and I know each other since our student days.~~

   ...........................................................................................................................................

2  ~~When arrived this fax?~~

   ...........................................................................................................................................

3  ~~How long do you have this office?~~

   ...........................................................................................................................................

4  ~~I haven't gone to the last conference.~~

   ...........................................................................................................................................

Points
/5

5  ~~I am part of the project team since last month.~~

   ...........................................................................................................................................

**F** Complete with the correct simple past or present perfect form.

1  When ........................ (**Max/join**) the company? And where ........................ (**he/work**)

   before that?

2  Mia ........................ (**be**) manager since Ken Tyson ........................ (**leave**) last year.

Points
/8

3  Sorry. I ........................ (**not have**) time to tell you before the meeting ........................ (**start**).

4  I ........................ (**speak**) to Rita earlier, but I ........................ (**not speak**) to Jason yet.

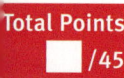
**Total Points**
/45

**A  Underline the correct forms.**

1  A taxi **drove** / **was driving** slowly up to the building, **stopped** / **was stopping** outside the main entrance, and two Arabs **got out** / **were getting out**.

2  By the end of the trip we **flew** / **had flown** over 8000 miles.

3  It was 11 p.m. and I **drove** / **was driving** home from Brussels. The autobahn **was** / **was being** empty. It **had been** / **has been** a long day.

4  I **have been writing** / **have written** up the minutes of yesterday's meeting for almost an hour now, but I still haven't finished.

5  Max **has been having** / **has had** a long discussion on the phone with the people in Manila and apparently all the problems are now resolved.

6  We **just talked** / **were just talking** about two of our colleagues when suddenly they **walked in** / **were walking in**.

7  What **did you do** / **were you doing** when I **saw** / **was seeing** you in the factory?

8  When I **looked** / **was looking** into Simon's office on the day of the product launch, people **drank and talk and had** / **were drinking and talking and having** a good time.

Points
☐ /15

**B  Complete the second sentence with the present perfect simple or progressive.**

1  What is going on? Mr Soames and Dr Wenzel ..................................... (talk) to each other over in the corner there for twenty minutes now.

2  I ..................................... (get) ready for my trip for some time. There's a lot to think about.

3  That electric car is apparently Martina's new company car. She ..................................... (only have) it a few days.

4  We joined the company in the same year. We ..................................... (know) each other for a long time.

5  I've heard that Nina is going to retire to the South of France. She ..................................... (always want) to do that.

6  I'm sorry I'm late. ..................................... (you/wait) for me?

7  He just doesn't listen. I ..................................... (tell) him a hundred times that he can't expect everyone to speak English.

8  Your Spanish sounds good to me. How long ..................................... (you/learn) it?

9  I need a break. I ..................................... (reply) to emails non-stop all morning.

10  Why don't we take them to the Thai restaurant? Frank ..................................... (often eat) there with guests.

Points
☐ /10

**C** Complete the conversations with the simple past and past progressive.

1 A: ........................ (you/hear) all that noise while we were in the presentation? It sounded as

though people ........................ (shout) all the time.

B: Yes, apparently there was a political demonstration.

2 A: Everybody ........................ (go) quiet as soon as I ........................ (enter) the room.

Why?

B: If you really want to know, they ........................ (discuss) your possible promotion.

**D** Complete the story with the correct past tenses.

Piotr is Polish, but he ...............................[1] (work) in Germany for several years now. He travels

between Essen and Cracow quite often. Over the past three or four years he ...........................[2]

(often fly) with a budget airline, but the last time he ...........................[3] (make) the journey,

it was by train. It ...............................[4] (take) a lot longer, but he ...........................[5]

(enjoy) it. He ...............................[6] (not allow) himself the luxury of a slow journey for a long

time, and ...............................[7] (forget) what a pleasure it can be to just sit back and watch the

world go by. It ...............................[8] (not be) all good of course. Between Hanover and Berlin

there was a group of senior citizens in his carriage. He ...............................[9] (doze) when they

...............................[10] (get on) – all sixteen of them. They were a more than lively

group and ...............................[11] (still talk and laugh) when the train finally

...............................[12] (arrive) in Berlin. But then things ...............................[13]

(become) quieter again. The train ...............................[14] (cross) the border into Poland, and

Piotr immediately ...............................[15] (feel) at home, something he ...........................[16]

(never feel) on any of his journeys by air. The train ...............................[17] (continue) on its way.

Piotr ...............................[18] (stare) out of the window for quite some time,

lost in thought, when he suddenly ...............................[19] (hear) a voice

he ...............................[20] (know). It was an old girlfriend of his from his student days.

They talked for the rest of the journey, and he ...............................[21] (find out) that she

...............................[22] (be) married for over four years and ...........................[23]

(have) two young children. They ...............................[24] (leave) the train together and

...............................[25] (say) goodbye. Piotr says he ...............................[26] (ask)

himself ever since whether he did the right thing to leave home and move to Germany.

This train trip ...............................[27] (be) at least six weeks ago, but since then Piotr

...............................[28] (be) a different person, quieter and much more thoughtful.

He ...............................[29] (not say) anything specific to me, but I have the feeling

he ...............................[30] (think) about going back.

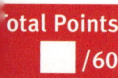

**A** Make sentences. There are always one or two words that you don't need.

1 a launch party for the new model / have / having / next Wednesday. / We're / will

..........................................................................................................

2 be / going to / is / Gloria / order / a new photocopier / soon.

..........................................................................................................

3 at 7.45. / goes / going / My flight / will

..........................................................................................................

4 be / Dr Cervantes / going to / I'll / next Tuesday. / seeing

..........................................................................................................

Points ☐ /4

**B** Underline the correct forms.

1 By this time tomorrow **I'll do** / **have done** the presentation.

2 My company **is sending** / **sends** me on a training course next month.

3 Can you call a bit later tomorrow? **I'll be** / **I am being** in a meeting till at least 10.30.

4 We've decided what **we're going to do** / **we'll have done** about the toxic waste.

5 I'm sorry, but I can't make Thursday. A delegation from Manila **will be visiting** / **will visit** us.

6 I promise you: nobody **is finding out** / **will find out** what we have discussed.

Points ☐ /6

**C** Correct the mistake. There may be more than one right answer.

1 What would you like? – ~~I just have a glass of water, please.~~ .............................................

2 We haven't decided yet, but perhaps ~~we sell the building.~~ .............................................

3 We need a new supplier. ~~I visit some possible firms~~ when I go to Latvia next month.

..........................................................................................................

4 ~~This time next month they have finished the new road.~~

..........................................................................................................

5 Orders are pouring in. If we're not careful, ~~we run out of stock.~~

..........................................................................................................

Points ☐ /5

**D** Complete with a future form. There may be more than one right answer.

A: So what are your plans for the weekend?

B: I ...............................[1] (go) to the sauna on Friday evening as usual. Then on Saturday

morning I ...............................[2] (take) someone to the airport. At the moment I don't

know what I ...............................[3] (do) for the rest of the time. What about you?

A: The weather forecast is not good. It ...............................[4] (be) cold and wet on

Saturday and Sunday. We ...............................[5] (probably stay) at home.

Points ☐ /5

Total Points ☐ /20

### A  Underline the correct forms.

1  The company's first shop  **is opened**  /  **was opened**  by the present owner's great-grandfather.

2  There has been a fire, and production  **is been**  /  **has been**  shut down.

3  The delegation  **will meet**  /  **will be met**  at the airport by Mr Li.

4  You can't use that room. Someone  **is being interviewed**  /  **is interviewed**  in there.

5  The report was written  **by**  /  **from**  Mr Molesworth.

Points
☐ /5

### B  Complete with the correct passive form.

Ladies and gentlemen, we are now entering the newest part of the factory complex. This building

.......................................[1] **(complete)** last year. Since then some new machines

.......................................[2] **(install)** and most of our top-range models

.......................................[3] **(now produce)** here. There is a control room from which

the production process can .......................................[4] **(view)**, but we can't get in today

because the room .......................................[5] **(re-equip)** with a new computer system.

Points
☐ /5

### C  Rewrite using the passive.

1  Make sure that someone informs the people in the next room.

Make sure that the people in the next room ......................................................

2  Has anyone made a reservation?

......................................................

3  We can't make any exceptions.

No exceptions ......................................................

4  People are making lots of complaints.

......................................................

5  Someone has taken the projector away.

......................................................

6  Someone reported the incident to the police.

......................................................

7  They'll probably give you a tour of the old city.

......................................................

8  They've asked me to organize the travel arrangements.

......................................................

9  They've offered Glenn the job.

......................................................

Points
☐ /10

10  What do we have to do next?

......................................................

**D** **Make a passive sentence that means the same.**

1 We are looking into various options.

   Various options ................................................................

2 They are trying out several new methods.

   ........................................................................

3 How will they pay for this massive new building programme?

   ........................................................................

4 When are they going to introduce the new system?

   ........................................................................

5 Did they introduce you to your key account manager?

   ........................................................................

Points /5

**E** **Complete with the passive infinitive or the passive gerund.**

1 I expect ............................ (inform) immediately when a problem like this occurs.

2 As a press officer you get used to ............................ (interview) and you also get used to

   ............................ (criticize).

3 I'm afraid of ............................ (give) jobs that I'm not really qualified to do.

4 Ann is fed up with ............................ (overlook) every time a higher position has to be filled.

   I think her chances of ............................ (offer) a job elsewhere would be good.

5 Can you imagine ............................ (pay) only once a year? I would refuse

   ............................ (employ) on that sort of basis.

6 Would you like ............................ (show) round the factory later on?

7 There's plenty of time. This doesn't have to ............................ (do) till next week.

Points /10

**F** **Make a second sentence that means the same, using the verb in brackets in the passive.**
There is a rumour that the CEO supports a different option. (understand)
*The CEO is understood to support a different option.*

1 People say that Malcolm will get the job. (expect)

   Malcolm ................................................................

2 Commentators believe that a strike is unavoidable. (think)

   A strike ................................................................

3 They say that the negotiators are personal friends. (believe)

   The negotiators ................................................................

4 It's no secret that the company donates money to the ruling party. (know)

   The company ................................................................

5 Sources suggest that an Arab prince is interested in the company. (say)

   An Arab prince ................................................................

Points /5

Total Points /40

109

**A** Complete the sentences with these verbs. Use each item once.

can • couldn't • didn't have to • don't have to • had to • have to • haven't been able to • must • mustn't • won't be able to

1 How did the meeting go? I'm sorry I ......................... get there on time.

2 I ....................... remember to inform everybody of the change of room.

3 I have a teleconference with Copenhagen at 12. I ....................... forget.

4 I missed my connecting flight . I ....................... wait six hours for the next one.

5 I am not fully in the picture. I ............................ answer your queries until I've read the report.

6 I'm expecting an urgent courier delivery. ........................ you let me know immediately it arrives?

7 I've done some internet searches, but I ....................... find out who is really behind the company.

8 My Chinese hosts arranged everything for me. I ....................... do anything.

9 The service is very easy to use. You ....................... register and you don't need a password either.

10 We can't wait much longer. We'll ....................... make a decision by the end of the week.

Points
☐ /10

**B** Circle all the possible right answers.

1 I don't know, but you ... need a visa. Have you checked on the internet?

   **A** can **B** may **C** might **D** will have to

2 The situation ... improve over the coming summer months, but it depends on several factors.

   **A** can **B** could **C** may **D** might

3 We ... leave for another 20 minutes. There's still plenty of time.

   **A** don't have to **B** mustn't **C** needn't **D** won't have to

4 We ... log on to the system because the password had been changed.

   **A** can't **B** couldn't **C** might not be able to **D** weren't able to

5 It says the result is a price rise of 8000%, but that's impossible. One of these figures ... be right.

   **A** can't **B** could **C** may not **D** might not

6 It's too late, we've missed our chance. We ... got the contract if we'd offered a lower price.

   **A** can have **B** could have **C** may have **D** might have

7 I didn't go to the conference so we ... had a meeting there.

   **A** can't have **B** couldn't have **C** may not have **D** might not have

8 You've made me look a complete idiot. You ... me of what was going to happen.

   **A** have had to warn **B** must have warned **C** ought to have warned **D** should have warned

9 Jason didn't join us for dinner. We waited for him, but we ... that.

   **A** didn't have to do **B** didn't must do **C** needn't do **D** needn't have done

Points
☐ /10

10 Nobody has met her yet, but our new colleague ... be over 60 years old.

   **A** shall **B** is said to **C** ought to **D** should

Total Points
☐ /20

**A** Match the parts. Write A–F in the boxes.

1  Have you been          **A**  going to apply?

2  Do you                 **B**  look at what I sent you?

3  Did you                **C**  able to contact Marcel?

4  Have you               **D**  at yesterday's briefing?

5  Are you                **E**  know Manila?

6  Were you               **F**  met before?

1 ☐  2 ☐  3 ☐  4 ☐  5 ☐  6 ☐

Points
☐ /6

**B** Complete these short answers to the questions in part **A** .

1  No, ...............................

2  Yes, ...............................

3  No, ...............................

4  Yes, ...............................

5  Yes, ...............................

6  No, ...............................

Points
☐ /6

**C** Write the questions.

A: Are you having a good time? How many people ..............................[1] **(you/know)** here?

B: Quite a few. I was at that Asian sales conference in Hong Kong last year.

A: Oh right. So who ...............................[2] **(you/meet)** there?

B: Sandra Hong, Mr Li, and several others.

A: Which department ...............................[3] **(Sandra / work in)**?

B: She's in R&D. ...............................[4] **(you/want)** me to introduce you?

Points
☐ /4

**D** Complete with the correct question tag.

1  I'm not asking too much, ........................?

2  Norbert sent out the invitations, ........................?

3  The seats weren't very comfortable, ........................?

4  It costs too much, ........................?

Points
☐ /4

Total Point
☐ /20

**A** Underline the correct forms.

1 Can you imagine **working** / **to work** from home all the time?

2 Have they finished **discussing** / **to discuss** the design yet?

3 I hope you don't mind **waiting** / **to wait** a little longer.

4 I'd like **visiting** / **to visit** the factory when I'm there.

5 I'll leave in plenty of time. I don't want to risk **being** / **to be** late.

6 If you're under pressure all the time, you can't avoid **making** / **to make** mistakes.

7 Jamie hopes **getting** / **to get** a pay rise.

8 Marie dislikes **working** / **to work** in an office on her own.

9 They offered **paying** / **to pay** for my flight.

Points
☐ /10

10 What do you suggest **doing** / **to do**?

**B** Fill in the correct preposition and gerund.

1 Have they succeeded ........................ **(find)** a successor for Diana yet?

2 I'm always afraid ........................ **(hurt)** his feelings if I say anything critical.

3 I'm not very good ........................ **(keep)** to deadlines.

4 I'm so tired ........................ **(hear)** the same old arguments.

5 Is there any chance ........................ **(find)** something to eat in this place?

6 Mrs Williams apologized ........................ **(forget)** to inform me.

7 Sheila has often talked ........................ **(go)** abroad.

8 The idea ........................ **(get)** a consultant in worries me.

Points
☐ /10

9 Mr Carmichael insists ........................ **(give)** the opening speech himself.

10 What were the reasons ........................ **(refuse)** the offer?

**C** Write sentences that mean the same, with a gerund.
We left the meeting. Then we had a quiet drink together. **(after)**
*After leaving the meeting we had a quiet drink together.*

1 Don't make a decision until you've checked all the options. **(before)**

........................................................................

2 Don't write emails that he never replies to. Why don't you phone him? **(instead of)**

........................................................................

3 The presenter continued. She didn't answer the question. **(without)**

........................................................................

Points
☐ /4

4 You can access some parts of the website only if you register. **(by)**

........................................................................

**D** **Make one sentence with a gerund or an infinitive.**

**1** I don't mind. I'll stay here all night if we can find a good solution.

I don't mind .......................... here all night if we can find a good solution.

**2** Georg asked me. So I bought a traditional doll for his daughter.

Georg asked me .......................... a traditional doll for his daughter.

**3** You can import as much currency as you like. They let you.

They let you ..............................................................................................

**4** Will we have regular meetings? Will it involve that?

Will it involve ...........................................................................................?

**5** The discussion is going round in circles. I'll go crazy if it carries on.

I'll go crazy if the discussion ...................................................................

**6** We can take part in the exhibition. We've been invited.

.................................................................................................................

**7** Don't eat in the old city. I wouldn't recommend it.

.................................................................................................................

**E** **Complete with a suitable verb as a gerund or an infinitive.**

| give • go • know • leave • postpone • share • spend • take • talk • try |
| --- |

**1** I'd love ........................ what went on behind those closed doors.

**2** I suggest ........................ a half-hour break.

**3** Will you please stop ........................ and listen!

**4** Will they let us ........................ work early?

**5** Mark has offered ........................ me a lift.

**6** Would you like ........................ some of our local wine?

**7** We've agreed ........................ the costs 50/50.

**8** I don't really enjoy ........................ on long business trips.

**9** Do you think they would consider ........................ the decision for two weeks?

**10** The new plan would involve ........................ an extra €200,000.

**F** **Complete with the gerund or infinitive.**

**1** A: Do you remember that horror trip to Kazachstan?

B: Yes. I remember ........................[1] (sit) in the airport lounge for hours!

A: I'll never forget ........................[2] (argue) with that taxi driver about the price.

**2** A: I meant ........................[3] (tell) you, Margaret can't attend the meeting.

B: That means ........................[4] (ask) someone else to give the progress report on the building work.

**A** **Underline the correct forms.**

1 If we're late, we can **easy** / **easily** get a taxi.

2 The antivirus program should update **automatic** / **automatically**.

3 How **expensive** / **expensively** was your hotel?

4 Maxine speaks both Polish and Czech **fluent** / **fluently**.

5 I can't visualize very **good** / **well**, I'm more an audio type.

6 Have you spoken to Astrid **late** / **lately**?

7 I feel really **happy** / **happily** that we signed the contract.

8 Simon's new job sounds **good** / **well**, don't you think?

9 Emma was **extreme** / **extremely** angry when I told her.

10 The phones have been **unusual** / **unusually** quiet for a Monday morning.

Points /10

**B** **Write a sentence that means the same. Use an adverb.**
Raoul is a *cautious* negotiator. **(negotiate)**
*Raoul negotiates cautiously.*

1 The traffic is very *slow* today. **(move)**

........................................................................................................

2 Elena's English is really *good*. **(speak)**

........................................................................................................

3 The conference is an *annual* event. **(take place)**

........................................................................................................

4 We had *heavy* rain all afternoon. **(rain)**

........................................................................................................

5 The train came to a *sudden* stop. **(stop)**

........................................................................................................

6 Frank said a *hurried* goodbye. **(leave)**

........................................................................................................

7 The representative from Prague was an *early* arrival. **(arrive)**

........................................................................................................

8 Martin was *angry* when I told him the news. **(react)**

........................................................................................................

9 Roanne gave a *nervous* laugh. **(laugh)**

........................................................................................................

Points /10

10 They lost two colleagues in the fire. It was *tragic*. **(die)**

........................................................................................................

**C** Complete with the correct form – adverb or adjective.

I'm Czech, but I work in a German company. We use English most of the time. I don't speak it

........................[1] (particular) ........................[2] (good), but my German is worse, so I wasn't

........................[3] (exact) looking forward to the teleconference we had in German last week. I

knew I would have to be very ........................[4] (attentive) and listen ........................[5]

(careful) to what everyone else was saying. But on the day I found that I could follow the discussion

........................[6] (relative) ........................[7] (easy), so my listening skills are

........................[8] (clear) better than I thought. But I must make a ........................[9] (serious)

effort to improve my speaking. The people could ........................[10] (hard) understand me!

Points
☐ /10

**D** Fill in the correct comparative or superlative form of the adjective.

1 The print is too small. The headings should be in a ........................ (big) size.

2 This is by far the ........................ (expensive) solution, but in the long term perhaps the best.

3 I must say that I feel ........................ (confident) than I did before the meeting.

4 This is one of the ........................ (busy) times of the year for us.

5 The big new window makes this office feel ........................ (airy) than it did.

6 It happened at the ........................ (less) expected moment.

7 What is the ........................ (hard) part of your job?

8 The company's headquarters are in the ........................ (tall) building in the city.

9 What is the ........................ (bad) experience you ever had?

10 One of the ........................ (surprising) developments has been the reduction in the price of oil.

Points
☐ /10

**E** Circle the right answer.

1 Birgit is ... .

   **A** as well-informed as I  **B** as well-informed as me  **C** as well-informed than I  **D** as well-informed than me

2 I thought the written test was ... the oral one.

   **A** easier as  **B** easier than  **C** easyer than  **D** more easy as

3 The location is not ideal for our new factory. The ... airport is over 100 kilometres away.

   **A** most near  **B** most next  **C** nearest  **D** next

4 You started on the the same day ..., didn't you?

   **A** as I  **B** as me  **C** like me  **D** than I

Points
☐ /4

**F** Mark the correct position for the adverb.

1 We [A] ...... go [B] ...... out for a drink after work. (often)
2 If you take the job, I expect you'll have to work [A] ...... late [B] ...... . (every day)
3 Jack is [A] ...... not coming [B] ...... to the meeting. (definitely)
4 Juliana solved [A] ...... the problem [B] ...... . (expertly)
5 They didn't [A] ...... organize the discussion [B] ...... . (very well)
6 We [A] ...... use [B] ...... a different company. (usually)

Points
☐ /6

Total Point
☐ /50

**A** **Underline the correct forms.**

1  What **equipment** / **equipments** does a technician need?

2  How **many damages** / **much damage** did the factory fire cause?

3  I need to write this down. Have you got **a paper** / **a piece of paper** for me?

4  I have a whole list of **work** / **works** to do today.

5  Slow progress **are** / **is** being made.

Points /5

**B** **Where does a belong? In position A or B? Mark the correct position.**

1  Susan may have [A] . . . . . . special tip for you. She always gives [B] . . . . . . good advice.

2  What [A] . . . . . . skyline! It looks even better in [B] . . . . . . weather like this.

3  The conference room was in [A] . . . . . . terrible state. It was [B] . . . . . . real chaos.

4  Megan speaks [A] . . . . . . fluent German. She doesn't speak with [B] . . . . . . British accent.

5  That is such [A] . . . . . . useful information. It's [B] . . . . . . real help.

Points /5

**C** **Complete with the correct item from the box.**

| any • piece of • many • much • some |
| --- |

1  Can you give me . . . . . . . . . . . . . . . . . . . . . . help, please?

2  I'm afraid I can't give you . . . . . . . . . . . . . . . . . . . . . . advice. I've never been in a situation like this.

3  This . . . . . . . . . . . . . . . . . . . . . . information is the key to it all.

4  We didn't make . . . . . . . . . . . . . . . . . . . . . . progress, but it was better than nothing.

5  There aren't . . . . . . . . . . . . . . . . . . . . . . journalists who have managed to get an interview with him.
He gives very few.

Points /5

**D** **Fill in is or are.**

1  . . . . . the United States still the biggest economy in the world?

2  My knowledge of this region . . . . . very limited.

3  Where . . . . . your glasses? Or do you have contact lenses now?

4  The news . . . . . not too good, I'm afraid.

5  Concrete information about this . . . . . hard to find, even on the internet.

6  Jeans . . . . . not appropriate clothing in many business situations.

7  The police . . . . . looking everywhere.

8  Five years . . . . . a very long time in the computer industry.

9  The old machinery . . . . . being replaced.

Points /10

10  Thanks . . . . . owed to all who have helped to make this event such a remarkable success.

Total Points /25

**A** Underline the correct forms.

1 She started her career as **a secretary** / **secretary** in a state tax office.

2 Do you know anything about **Indian history** / **the Indian history**?

3 Do you know anything about **history** / **the history** of India?

4 Mr Li is **a smoker** / **smoker** like many of his colleagues.

5 **Life** / **The life** for many of these migrant workers is very hard.

6 The CEO's death was **a such** / **such a** shock.

7 I was born in a town in **Austrian Alps** / **the Austrian Alps**.

8 We stayed in Manhattan in a hotel near **Central Park** / **the Central Park**.

9 The strike is costing us €200,000 **a** / **the** day.

10 I have **a terrible** / **terrible** headache.

Points ☐ /10

**B** Complete with **some**, **any** or a compound with **some** or **any** (e.g. **someone**).

1 Can you turn on the light, please? I can't see ........................

2 Everything is under control. There isn't ........................ you have to do.

3 I don't have ........................ idea how high transport costs are likely to be.

4 Let's go ........................ nice. How about that restaurant by the river?

5 Let's have ........................ coffee, shall we?

6 No, you can't go in, sorry. She's too busy to talk to ........................

7 Martin has ........................ with him who knows Singapore well.

8 This is ridiculous. There must be ........................ they can do to stop this.

9 We never have ........................ real discussions.

10 Can I offer you ........................ of this wine?

Points ☐ /10

**C** Circle the right answer.

1 Birgit is the computer expert ... . Don't you remember?

   **A** I talked to  **B** to that I talked  **C** to who I talked  **D** which I talked to

2 We've not heard from them since we sent the new designs ... .

   **A** what is unusual  **B** , what is unusual  **C** which is unusual  **D** , which is unusual

3 About 50 people were at the presentation, ... were experts on the subject.

   **A** most of whom  **B** of who most  **C** of who the most  **D** the most of whom

4 Janan and I have known ... for over 15 years.

   **A** each other  **B** ourselves  **C** us  **D** we

5 Timothy and Bettina ... at a seminar and got married last month.

   **A** met  **B** met them  **C** met themself  **D** met themselves

Points ☐ /5

Total Points ☐ /25

**A** **Underline the correct forms.**

1 I would have dropped by if I **had had** / **would have** time.

2 If Mr Li **calls** / **will call,** tell him I will call back later.

3 If nothing happens soon, **I make** / **I'll make** an official complaint.

4 If there **is** / **will be** a delay, I'll send you a text.

5 If we changed our provider, it **saved** / **would save** a lot of money.

6 If we had known how difficult it is to find accommodation, we **hadn't** / **wouldn't have** left it so late to book something.

7 If you **ever needed** / **would ever need** help, I'm sure you could ask Rebecca.

8 What would you do if you **were** / **would be** in my position?

9 You **didn't** / **wouldn't** make mistakes like this if you took more time.

10 You wouldn't be able to rent a place like this if you **lived** / **would live** in Germany.

Points ☐ /10

**B** **Complete with the correct form.**

1 A: Where are you going to base your business?

   B: We don't know yet, but if we can find affordable office space in the centre of town, we
   .............................. (take) that. If we .............................. (not find) anything
   suitable, we'll work from home initially.

   A: If I was setting up a business, I .............................. (not want) to do that.

2 A: You must be glad that you didn't go to that conference.

   B: You can say that again. It .............................. (be) a complete waste of time if
   I .............................. (go).

   A: You .............................. (not get) much out of it.

3 A: I .............................. (take) you to the airport if you .............................. (like).

   B: That's very kind of you. Thanks very much. But the flight is quite early, at 8.10.

   A: That's OK. If you .............................. (not hear) anything further from me, I
   .............................. (pick) you up at your hotel at 6.45.

4 A: If you .............................. (have) the chance of working abroad, would you take it?

   B: It would depend on the country. If it .............................. (be) a country where they speak
   English, I .............................. (go).

5 A: How much demand is there for this sort of service?

   B: Well, let's say that if we could be certain of finding 2000 customers, we ..............................
   (go) ahead with the idea.

Points ☐ /15

   A: 2000 is a lot. If you got 1200 to start with, .............................. (that / not be) enough?

## C Circle the right answer.

**1** If I'd known they were going to be so late, I ... with some other work.

    **A** could get on   **B** can have got on   **C** got on   **D** would have got on

**2** This muddle ... if you had checked with me first.

    **A** didn't happen   **B** hadn't happened   **C** wouldn't happen   **D** wouldn't have happened

**3** If you ... from me for another two weeks, please don't think I'm not interested. I will have to clarify things with my superiors and that will take time.

    **A** didn't hear   **B** don't hear   **C** won't hear   **D** wouldn't hear

**4** If we ... more time, we could do this job better.

    **A** had   **B** have   **C** will have   **D** would have

**5** If a customer ... too much, would you tell them?

    **A** pay   **B** paid   **C** would pay   **D** would paid

**6** What ... if they offered you the position? I'm not sure that it's so attractive.

    **A** said you   **B** will you say   **C** would you have said   **D** would you say

**7** If you ... Isabella Walters, say hello to her from me.

    **A** saw   **B** see   **C** will see   **D** would see

**8** Their new initiative was totally unexpected. If I had been expecting it, I ... prepare a response.

    **A** was able to   **B** were able to   **C** would be able to   **D** would have been able to

**9** They were on the point of accepting our terms, and if you ... that stupid remark, we would have an agreement now.

    **A** didn't make   **B** hadn't made   **C** won't make   **D** wouldn't have made

**10** If I ... her better, I would have understood what she was trying to do.

    **A** know   **B** knew   **C** will know   **D** would know

Points
 /10

Total Point
/35

119

## Index A – Z

Hier finden Sie eine Liste mit grammatikalischen Begriffen in Deutsch und Englisch. Diese Liste geht über das Inhaltsverzeichnis hinaus, weil sie alle Seiten aufführt, auf denen eine Grammatikstruktur behandelt wird. Außerdem finden Sie Verweise auf einzelne Wörter, sowohl im Englischen als auch im Deutschen.

Deutsche Bezeichnungen für Grammatikstrukturen sind *fett kursiv* gedruckt, englische **fett**. Englische Stichwörter sind normal gedruckt und deutsche Stichwörter *kursiv*.
Die Zahlen verweisen jeweils auf die Seitenzahlen im Buch.

# Englische Grammatikbegriffe und ihre deutschen Übersetzungen

| | | | |
|---|---|---|---|
| active | *Aktiv, Tatform* | object | *Objekt, Satzergänzung* |
| adjective | *Adjektiv, Eigenschaftswort* | direct object | *direktes Objekt* |
| comparison of adjectives | *Steigerung von Adjektiven* | indirect object | *indirektes Objekt* |
| adverb | *Adverb, Umstandswort* | participle | *Partizip* |
| adverb of frequency | *Adverb der Häufigkeit* | past participle | *Partizip Perfekt* |
| comparison of adverbs | *Steigerung von Adverbien* | passive | *Passiv, Leideform* |
| position of adverbs | *Stellung von Adverbien* | passive progressive/ | |
| answer | *Antwort* | continuous | *Verlaufsform des Passivs* |
| short answer | *Kurzantwort* | past | *Vergangenheit* |
| article | *Artikel, Geschlechtswort* | past progressive/ | |
| definite article | *bestimmter Arikel* | continuous | *Verlaufsform der* |
| indefinite article | *unbestimmter Arikel* | | *Vergangenheit* |
| backshifting of tenses | *Zeitenverschiebung (bei der* | past perfect | *Past Perfect, Vorvergangenheit* |
| | *indirekten Rede)* | simple past | *einfache Vergangenheit* |
| comma | *Komma* | preposition | *Präposition, Verhältniswort* |
| conditional | *Bedingungsform, Konditional* | present | *Gegenwart* |
| conditional sentence | *Bedingungssatz,* | present progressive/ | |
| | *Konditionalsatz* | continuous | *Verlaufsform der Gegenwart* |
| continuous form | *Verlaufsform* | present perfect | *Present Perfect, Perfekt* |
| clause | *Teilsatz* | simple present | *einfache Gegenwart* |
| contact clause | *Relativsatz ohne* | progressive form | *Verlaufsform* |
| | *Relativpronomen* | pronoun | *Pronomen, Fürwort* |
| relative clause | *Relativsatz* | reflexive pronoun | *Reflexivpronomen* |
| future | *Futur, Zukunft* | relative pronoun | *Relativpronomen* |
| future progressive/ | | proper names | *Eigennamen* |
| continuous | *Verlaufsform des Futurs* | quantifiers | *Mengenangaben* |
| future perfect | *vollendete Zukunft* | question | *Frage* |
| gerund | *Gerundium* | question tag | *Frageanhängsel* |
| if-sentences | *If-Sätze* | question word | *Fragewort* |
| indirect speech | *indirekte Rede, berichtete* | relative clause | *Relativsatz* |
| | *Rede* | non-defining relative | *nicht bestimmender* |
| infinitive | *Infinitiv, Grundform* | clause | *Relativsatz* |
| passive infinitive | *Infinitivform des Passivs* | defining relative clause | *bestimmender Relativsatz* |
| -ing form | *-ing-Form* | reported speech | *indirekte Rede, berichtete* |
| negation | *Verneinung* | | *Rede* |
| noun | *Nomen, Substantiv,* | subject | *Subjekt, Satzgegenstand* |
| | *Hauptwort* | verb | *Verb, Tätigkeitswort* |
| abstract noun | *abstraktes Nomen* | irregular verb | *unregelmäßiges Verb* |
| countable noun | *zählbares Nomen* | modal verb | *Modalverb* |
| plural noun | *Mehrzahlnomen* | regular verb | *regelmäßiges Verb* |
| singular noun | *Einzahlnomen* | reflexive verb | *reflexives Verb* |
| uncountable noun | *nichtzählbares Nomen* | | |

# Schreibbesonderheiten

Die Schreibweise eines Wortes kann sich abhängig von der anzuhängenden Endung ändern.

### Endung -s wird zu -es (Unit 1)
■ Endet ein Wort auf -s, -ss, -sh, -ch oder -x, so wird vor der Endung -s
ein zusätzliches e eingesetzt.
kiss ⸱⸱⸱⟩ kiss**es**, wash ⸱⸱⸱⟩ wash**es**, watch ⸱⸱⸱⟩ watch**es**, fix ⸱⸱⸱⟩ fix**es**

### Stummes -e entfällt (Units 2, 5, 6, 7, 29, 37)
■ Endet ein Wort auf ein stummes -e, so entfällt das -e vor den Endungen -ing,
-ed, -er/-est.
make ⸱⸱⸱⟩ **making**, hope ⸱⸱⸱⟩ **hoping**, use ⸱⸱⸱⟩ **using**
hope ⸱⸱⸱⟩ **hoped**, use ⸱⸱⸱⟩ **used**, smoke ⸱⸱⸱⟩ **smoked**
white ⸱⸱⸱⟩ **whiter/whitest**, wide ⸱⸱⸱⟩ **wider/widest**

### Verdoppelung von Endkonsonanten (Units 2, 5, 6, 7, 29, 37)
■ Endet ein Wort auf einen (einzelnen) Vokal + einen (einzelnen) Konsonanten,
so wird der Konsonant vor den Endungen -ing, -ed, -er/-est verdoppelt, wenn:
– das Wort nur eine Silbe hat.
plan ⸱⸱⸱⟩ **planning**, stop ⸱⸱⸱⟩ **stopping**
plan ⸱⸱⸱⟩ **planned**, stop ⸱⸱⸱⟩ **stopped**
big ⸱⸱⸱⟩ **bigger/biggest**, hot ⸱⸱⸱⟩ **hotter/hottest**
Ausnahme: Vokal + w/y/x:
blow ⸱⸱⸱⟩ **blowing**, pay ⸱⸱⸱⟩ **paying**, fix ⸱⸱⸱⟩ **fixing**
low ⸱⸱⸱⟩ **lower/lowest**, stay ⸱⸱⸱⟩ **stayed**, fax ⸱⸱⸱⟩ **faxed**

– das Wort mehrsilbig ist und die Betonung auf der letzten Silbe liegt.
beGIN ⸱⸱⸱⟩ beGINNing, forGET ⸱⸱⸱⟩ forGETTing, conTROL ⸱⸱⸱⟩ conTROLLing
preFER ⸱⸱⸱⟩ preFERRed, conTROL ⸱⸱⸱⟩ conTROLLed
Ausnahme im britschen Englisch:
travel ⸱⸱⸱⟩ **travelling, travelled** (trotz Betonung auf der ersten Silbe)

### -y wird zu -i (Units 1, 5, 7, 36, 37)
■ Endet ein Wort auf einen Konsonanten + -y, so wird -y zu -i bzw. zu -ie vor den
Endungen -s, -ed, -er/-est, -ly (nicht aber vor -ing).
hurry ⸱⸱⸱⟩ **hurries**, try ⸱⸱⸱⟩ **tries**
hurry ⸱⸱⸱⟩ **hurried**, try ⸱⸱⸱⟩ **tried**
dry ⸱⸱⸱⟩ **drier/driest**, easy ⸱⸱⸱⟩ **easier/easiest**
busy ⸱⸱⸱⟩ **busily**, easy ⸱⸱⸱⟩ **easily**, lucky ⸱⸱⸱⟩ **luckily**

### -le entfällt vor -ly (Unit 36)
■ Endet ein Adjektiv auf -le, so entfällt -le vor -ly.
probable ⸱⸱⸱⟩ **probably**, simple ⸱⸱⸱⟩ **simply**

### -ic wird zu -ical vor -ly (Unit 36)
■ Endet ein Adjektiv auf -ic, so wird -ic + -ly zu -ically.
tragic ⸱⸱⸱⟩ **tragically**, automatic ⸱⸱⸱⟩ **automatically**